Valley of the Shadow

Valley of the Shadow

a journey through cancer and beyond

Gay J. Lindquist

iUniverse, Inc.
New York   Bloomington

Valley of the Shadow
A Journey Through Cancer and Beyond

Copyright © 2010 Gay J. Lindquist

iUniverse books may be ordered through booksellers or by contacting:

iUniverse
1663 Liberty Drive
Bloomington, IN 47403
www.iuniverse.com
1-800-Authors (1-800-288-4677)

ISBN: 978-1-4401-9675-1 (pbk)
ISBN: 978-1-4401-9677-5 (cloth)
ISBN: 978-1-4401-9676-8 (ebook)

Printed in the United States of America

iUniverse rev. date: 1/12/10

For my extraordinary family

Wayne,
Eric and Susan,
Katie and Jackson

and

for all those who journey with cancer

The Lord is my Shepherd; I shall not want.
He maketh me to lie down in green pastures:
He leadeth me beside the still waters.
He restoreth my soul:
He leadeth me in the paths of righteousness for his name's sake.
Yea, though I walk through the valley of the shadow of death,
I will fear no evil:
for thou art with me;
Thy rod and thy staff they comfort me.
Thou preparest a table before me in the presence of mine enemies:
thou anointest my head with oil;
My cup runneth over.
Surely goodness and mercy shall follow me all the days of my life:
and I will dwell in the house of the Lord forever.

Psalm 23, KJV

CONTENTS

PREFACE

It's a bright, sunny Florida morning, and I'm sitting on the lanai in our little winter home, feeling the warmth of the sun, looking out at the lush, tropical landscape—and remembering. I have just celebrated my seventy-first birthday, and my mind returns to this time eleven years ago when I began my journey with cancer. It was one of those difficult, challenging times of life, and even though I have never been very good at regularly keeping a journal, I did during that time. Unfortunately, somehow, both the print copy and the document on my computer were lost when we moved and our computer's hard drive crashed. Perhaps I should have been glad they were gone. I could have tried to forget and just put that period behind me, but for some reason I have a deep need to re-create that time. "Why?" you may ask. In part, I'm sure it is just a personal need to remember, but, also, I can't let go of the overwhelming feeling that I should do something with that whole experience. As painful as many of these memories are, there are things to be learned from them. The experience taught me to be more sensitive as I respond to friends and relatives experiencing health crises, and, by reliving this period and writing this memoir, I believe more can be learned, certainly by me, but perhaps also by others going through the experience of diagnosis and treatment of cancer.

I'm a retired nursing educator, but it should be clear from the outset that this is not written primarily from the perspective of a health care provider. There is no intent to provide medical information; this is, instead, simply a record of my memories of personal experiences and an attempt to learn from them. During that time I found it reassuring to know that someone else had experienced feelings similar to mine. It helped me to know that I wasn't crazy. Also, family members and friends of people dealing with cancer may learn something from my experiences that can help them to provide support to their loved ones and to care for themselves.

Even though my journals are lost, I find it amazingly easy to remember as I look at my calendar and a photo album from that time, and just let my mind go. I realize, however, that memory is a tricky thing. Some things I may have repressed, and my family and friends may have recollections very different from my own; still, these are my memories of my journey through cancer, and my survival. I invite you to travel with me as I reflect on that journey. Along the way, I will pause at several "waysides" in order to consider where I've been, what I have learned, and how it has continued to influence my journey through life.

CHAPTER ONE

Forewarning

October 1997

It was a gorgeous fall day, with the sun's rays still warm on our backs in the late afternoon. The reds and golds of the leaves reflected in the river as we looked down from the bridge. My husband, Wayne, and I were returning to our Eau Claire, Wisconsin, apartment with a dirty, giggling three-and-a-half year old Katie from the park across the river. We were all enjoying one of the regular Wednesdays our granddaughter spent with us. It was such a good point in our lives, for we were both relatively young and recently retired. We had a comfortable apartment in Eau Claire, a home we loved on Madeline Island in Lake Superior, a granddaughter we adored who unconditionally reciprocated our affection, and a second grandchild on the way. We weren't bound by a schedule and could travel when we wanted, as long as the budget allowed. Life couldn't have been better!

Oh, and did I say we were healthy? Though we were both somewhat overweight and I was starting to have a few joint problems, for the most part, we were healthy. What more could anyone ask? I didn't even have a cold. But as we walked across the bridge, I coughed. Nothing to even think about. We all cough sometimes, so I don't really know why, but I spit into a tissue and saw blood—not a little blood-tinged mucous like you see with irritated mucous membranes, but a small, formed globule. It seemed a little strange, but I stuck the tissue in the pocket of my jeans and walked on, laughing, across the bridge.

December 1997–January 1998

I don't remember the specifics of any similar episodes, just that there were a few of them—always far apart, just once, and then not again for several weeks. We were caught up in busy lives that were filled with volunteer activities, friends, our family, and planning for a new grandchild. Then it was Christmas, and what a wonderful Christmas it was! Eric, our son; his wife, Susie; and Katie came to the island and brought Susie's mom with them. Wayne had put sparkling colored lights all around the outside of the house, and Christmas lights twinkled in the pines in the driveway circle. Our tree was decorated with the ornaments we had collected from all over Europe in our travels, and it brought back wonderful memories of trips with Eric as a child and of Christmases past. I had so much fun decorating, feeling nostalgic as I placed some of my parents' favorite decorations around the hexagon-shaped house Wayne and I had built on our own years earlier. We built fires in the huge stone fireplace, lights glittered in and reflected on all of the windows, and the mantle was covered with fresh pine and big red pillar candles. The house was filled with the smell of pine and Christmas cookies baking as we made our traditional Scandinavian Christmas Eve dinner, and I covered the table with my favorite, festive holiday tablecloth. On Christmas Eve, Katie looked beautiful in her navy velvet dress, trimmed with white lace and a red rose, and Christmas morning was filled with excitement as she eagerly opened her gifts from Santa and the family. A few gifts were special that year. Eric and Susie gave us the "Welcome to the Island" sign that still hangs in the entryway, and we gave Katie a beautiful dollhouse that Wayne had lovingly built for her. It was a two-story Victorian with carpet on the stairs and wallpaper on the walls.

Dollhouse

Katie with Doll Family

She beamed as she sat on the floor beside it in her fuzzy pink sleeper and played with the tiny doll family and miniature furniture. Mandy, our blue-point Siamese, played among the wrappings while we opened gifts. Then, after scurrying around to pick up wrappings, we cooked the Christmas ham, set the table with linen and good china, and decorated it with red candles and cheery British Christmas crackers filled with jokes, crowns, and silly prizes. Friends joined us for Christmas dinner, and we all wore our flimsy paper Christmas crowns while we ate and laughed a lot. There was just enough snow to cover everything with a soft layer of white, and we all went for a walk through the silent, winter wonderland and took pictures out by the Lindquist sign at the end of our driveway.

Katie with Grandma Cathy and Grandma Gay

Eric, Susie, and Katie

It was a lovely, happy Christmas, filled with hope and eagerness for the new child who was to join our family in a few months. Somewhere in the midst of the celebrations I remember coughing up a little blood again, but it didn't seem significant, and it certainly didn't dampen my spirits for the holiday. Then a few days later, I did it again. Somewhere, way in the back of my mind, but moving a little closer to the surface, was a dark cloud, a bit of fear and foreboding mixed in with the joy—but then everything seemed fine. No more blood.

Eric and his family went home, but Wayne and I stayed on for a few days just to relax and enjoy our house and the peace and beauty of the island. We were tired and enjoyed the quiet and solitude after all of the excitement during the past week. Marina, our friend and pastor, invited us over for a dinner party one evening. I didn't cough up more blood, but it seemed like my airway was constricted. It was difficult not to wheeze. I don't remember what everyone talked about, just that it was an interesting topic, and normally I would have been engaged in the conversation, but this evening I couldn't concentrate. I asked myself, *Why is it hard to breathe? Why did I cough up blood?* I still don't know what the difficulty in breathing was about. I really never had problems with that again, but it frightened me. The next morning, when Wayne went to town, I got out a book in which you could look up symptoms and follow a chart showing what might be the cause of the symptom and what to do about it. So—cough up blood. Simple to find. Not the usual number of paths and possibilities to follow. Just two possible causes listed: tuberculosis or lung cancer. What to do? See doctor immediately. My mind raced. There had to be other possible explanations. I had smoked over a period of twenty-five years, but also had kicked the habit a decade earlier, and had quit several times during the years I smoked—one time even for seven years. *It can't be lung cancer,* I thought. *No! Not that! Tuberculosis? Not likely. But wait!* We had guests in late October, and I remembered them telling us they had learned that a friend they had visited had since been diagnosed with TB. *Could they have passed it on to me?* My logical nurse's mind said, *No, of course not; that is ridiculous, Gay. Tuberculosis can't be spread that way. But… maybe. Some really freaky thing may have happened. It could be,* I told myself.

Then it was New Year's Eve morning. We were going to an island New Year's Eve party that night, and I was looking forward to it. I had not yet said anything to Wayne about any of my symptoms, for it was Christmas, after all. Then, while we were sitting in bed watching TV and drinking coffee, I coughed. I felt that now-familiar feel of a little nodule of blood in my mouth. I spit into a tissue, and yes, it was blood. Then there was more, but now it was liquid. I spit, I spit again. More blood. Wayne asked what was wrong. I told him. I had to. I couldn't deny it anymore. Something was wrong. I was scared. There was more blood, and more, and I thought, *I'm on an island in Lake Superior! What if it won't stop?!? What will we do?* But it did. "You have to go and see a doctor!" Wayne declared.

"I will," I promised, "as soon as we get back to Eau Claire."

"OK," he replied hesitantly. "Are you sure we shouldn't go back today?"

"I'm positive!" I said. "I'm OK. I just want to stay on the island a few more days. Then I promise I'll go in."

I felt fine, as I had the entire time. There were no other symptoms and no more difficulty breathing, but all day I was afraid it would happen again. It didn't; there was no more blood. We went to the party, and I had a good time in spite of some apprehension. There were even moments at a time when I didn't think about it. But it was always there, lurking in the back of my mind. And I wondered—*What lies ahead?*

We stayed on the island for a few more days after New Year's. I was on the council at our local church, and on Saturday morning I had a budget meeting, after which some of us went out for lunch at the one restaurant open in our little island town that time of year. That evening we went to some good friends' home for dinner, and as we sat in their great room talking, laughing, and eating, looking out at quiet, peaceful, snow-covered Lake Superior, I tried to act *normal.* Inside, however, I experienced an undercurrent of feelings that felt like the cold, turbulent water hidden under the ice. Tomorrow we were returning to Eau Claire. *What will I face when we get there?* I asked silently. I didn't want to know.

CHAPTER TWO

Diagnosis

January 1998

The next afternoon we returned to Eau Claire, but I waited until morning to call the clinic. I was not able to get in to see Sue, my regular physician, so I made an appointment with someone else, someone I'd never seen before. It seemed that the time in the waiting room was endless, but finally my name was called, and I followed a nurse to an exam room. When the physician entered the room, he seemed to be in a hurry and rather uninterested in the fact that I was coughing up blood. He asked a few questions about smoking history, earlier respiratory ailments, and a few other things, and then said, "It's probably just an allergy, nothing to be concerned about." *An allergy*, I thought. *That could tie in with the one evening I felt like my airway was constricted. Ahh! Allergy pills and it can be all fixed.* But, he added, "Just to be on the safe side we should get a chest X-ray." So I went down to X-ray. I don't really remember anything in particular about having the X-ray taken, just going back upstairs clutching an oversized manila envelope containing pictures of my chest. It was hard to resist the urge to take them out and hold them up to the light to see if I could see anything unusual, but it wasn't the appropriate thing to do, so, compliant patient that I was, I just

8

sat there—waiting. It seemed like hours, but I suppose in reality it was only minutes. I vividly remember looking at the picture of Glenn Giffen, my old physician and friend. He was sitting by a stream in the woods, wearing a plaid shirt, looking very peaceful. But his picture was there because he is no longer at the clinic. He is dead—from cancer—at far too young an age, so I could gain no reassurance from my old friend, only an increasing sense of anxiety.

Finally, my name was called, and I walked toward the exam room door. My feet didn't want to carry me down the hallway. They wanted to turn and run. Surely, not knowing would be better than what I might hear on the other side of that door! I walked hesitantly into the exam room and sat tremulously, listening to my heart hammering in my ears. Waiting. A few moments later the physician appeared with the envelope holding my X-rays. The first thing I noticed was that he wouldn't look me in the eye. He just kept looking down at the envelope he held in his hands. I felt a sense of growing dread. "There's a mass in the right lower lobe of your lung," he told me as he busied himself removing the X-rays and placing them on the view box in the room. *Mass!* I expected to see something huge, and could barely see the tiny spot he pointed out to me. I'm really not sure exactly what he told me. He probably said it could be something else, but I think that he said it was most likely cancer, and that I should see a pulmonologist. He must have offered some words of reassurance, but I can't recall them. I just remember feeling that I had kind of ruined his day—someone who wasn't his regular patient coming in with a mass in her chest.

The next thing I remember is sitting in a chair at the reappointment desk. The clerk seemed so matter of fact about it, as if it were just a regular referral, which, of course it was, to her. She called the pulmonary clinic and said, "I have a patient with a *mass* in her chest." She seemed to say it so loud. *Be quiet,* I wanted to shout. *It has to be a mistake! I don't want the whole world to know!* I don't know if this would be true with other types of cancer, but because it was lung cancer, I felt incredibly guilty. I *had* smoked. I had started at a time when all the articles and the health warnings on packs of cigarettes weren't there for everyone to see, but still I should have known better. I wasn't a kid; I was a nursing student, a rule-abiding, clean-cut, all-American, Iowa farm girl who was perhaps having some kind of delayed adolescent rebellion. *You did quit, though, many years ago*, I told myself, *and without all the helpful aids that are available now!* But that didn't help. I still felt guilty—and ashamed. If it was cancer, and I suppose some part of me was quite sure it was, I had brought it on myself. The next thing I knew I had an appointment with a pulmonologist at the end of the week. I walked down the stairs of the clinic and out to my car feeling as if I were engulfed in a heavy blanket of fog. It muted everything and made it seem unreal. I was a health care provider, not a cancer patient! *This can't be happening*, I thought, but I looked at the appointment slip in my hand and saw only the word *pulmonologist* jump out at me. There was a mass in my chest—but it was so tiny! *Surely it can't be cancer*, I thought. *Surely not!*

Next I had to think about how to tell Wayne. *I can't*, I thought simply. *I just can't do this!* I got in my car and pulled out of the parking lot, but instead of turning toward home, I turned the opposite direction. I drove through Carson Park, stopping to look out over Half Moon Lake. The tears streamed down my cheeks as I cried out to myself, *How can this be? How can I face this?* I remembered Jan, my dear friend, who had died from lung cancer only three and a half years earlier, and the tears continued to fall. The lake looked so peaceful, surrounded by snow. How I longed to absorb some of that peace! I prayed, just for strength—strength to tell Wayne, strength to see me through whatever lay ahead. I just sat there, quietly, and then, finally, knowing that I had been gone much longer than Wayne expected, I turned my car toward home.

I don't need calendars or photo albums to jog my memory about what it was like to walk in that door. He was standing in the kitchen, getting something ready for lunch. "What did he say?" he asked. I could see he was anxious, but I also knew that he was totally unprepared for what I was about to say.

I didn't know how to soft-pedal it. I took a deep breath and said, "They took a chest X-ray … It showed a mass." His face mirrored mine as I said the word. It's such a revolting word! It sounds huge! Once I had said that horrid word, I could begin to try to reassure him. I paused and finally added, "It was small … and isn't necessarily cancer. It could be other things." Then we tried to reassure each other, but, internally, we both knew that it could be cancer—the big C word that we all go through life fearing. Cancer, the disease that had killed Jan.

In my memory, everything from this point on revolved around appointments with physicians and tests, and it all went on forever, but when I pulled out an old calendar, I was reminded that's not the way it was at all. Life went on—filled with meetings, lunches and dinners with friends, Wednesdays with Katie, concerts and plays in Minneapolis and St. Paul. We saw many people, but I still didn't tell anyone else my dark secret.

It seemed like a long week, but Friday finally arrived and we went to see the pulmonologist. He was very kind as he said, "I looked at your films, but there is no way to make a diagnosis without further tests." Then he scheduled pulmonary function tests, a CAT scan, and a bronchoscopy for the next week. "I'm afraid lung cancer is likely," he added, "but remember, there are other possibilities." Sarcoidosis, an inflammatory disease that often affects the lungs, was one of the conditions he mentioned. *Oh!* I thought. *Mom had that. Maybe it runs in families! We know other people that have it, too. That's not so rare. It doesn't kill you.* Then he mentioned that silicosis can be caused by the dust in cat litter. *That must be it,* I thought! I think Wayne started cleaning the cat litter box then and has almost always since. It's strange, when you think about it. If I already had it, why wouldn't we have wanted to protect him instead of me? Perhaps we weren't thinking terribly clearly just then.

But life went on. We drove to the island for a church council meeting, then on to Minneapolis-St. Paul to visit our friends, Pat and Heidi, and to attend a St. Paul Chamber Orchestra concert. I hadn't wanted to tell anyone, but especially not Pat. After all, Jan, his first wife, had died only a few years earlier from lung cancer. I could still hear Jan cough in my mind. I could see her deteriorate—so rapidly. I remembered her writing her own memorial service. I could hear the haunting flute music she chose for her service. *Oh, Jan! Why did you have to die?* I cried in my heart. *I can't be next! I'm not ready!* But, of course, she wasn't *ready* either. Then I remembered, with a chill, that she had died just before her second grandchild was born, and I pictured Susie and Andi, their daughter, standing in their navy blue maternity dresses, "belly to belly" after her memorial service. *My second grandchild is due soon. I can't die, too! Not yet.*

As the week went on, our calendar continues to show that we did normal things. We went out with friends and cared for Katie, but I was always thinking about what I was going to learn from the scheduled tests, even though I couldn't talk about it. As I laughed and talked with friends, I would ask myself, *Does anyone suspect? Does anyone notice that something is wrong?* I still don't know. I suppose we all become absorbed in our own lives and don't notice little signs that something is troubling someone else.

Then it was time to begin the tests, the first of which was the CAT scan. As I sat in the X-ray waiting room, I found it impossible to concentrate on the book that I had carried along. I picked up a magazine instead, leafing through the pages, absorbing absolutely nothing. All I could think about was what would show up in the images about to be captured on the scan. I looked at the people around me. There was an emaciated woman in a wheelchair with a scarf tied around her apparently bald head, with a tired-looking elderly man sitting next to her, staring down at his hands. Several people sat with intravenous drips and poles attached to their wheelchairs, one a pale, thin young man with a baseball cap covering his bald head. Everyone looked *sick!* There must have been others as well, young athletes with sports injuries and healthy people with casts and broken limbs, but I can only recall those who looked like cancer patients—the ones who made me terrified of my own future and what it might hold. Finally, I heard my name being called and I obediently walked toward a young, smiling technician with whom I chatted about normal things. I felt, for a few moments, a little bit more like a health care professional, and not quite so much like a frightened patient. However, as I stripped to the waist, I also stripped away any facade of normalcy, and there was no doubt that I was *the patient.*

I had worked in and around hospitals for years but had never seen a CAT scan machine. It looked like an enormous monster with a narrow cot sticking out of its gaping center hole. I followed the technician's instructions and lay down on the hard surface extending from the machine, trying to take deep cleansing breaths as I looked up at the opening in the machine above my head. She covered me with warm blankets and stuck a needle in my arm for an intravenous drip. Before she injected the dye, she explained, "Almost as soon as I inject this you will feel an overall hot, flushing feeling. You will also feel a strange, but very real, sensation that you are peeing your pants." Then she asked, "Have you ever had any difficulty with claustrophobia?"

I quickly replied, "Yes!" recalling my panic attack while working in the crawl space under our house several years earlier.

"Don't worry," she added reassuringly. "You will be moved in slowly, and the machine will stop when it reaches your neck. Your head will not go into the machine." The cot started to move, and as it reached my chest, I listened to the strange whirring sounds of the machine. My mind whirred along with the machine as I listened to the sounds and wondered what the pictures would show. Just as I was about to panic, thinking that somehow they had forgotten to stop the machine and that my head was going to go inside, it all stopped—the movement, the noise. There was just an eerie silence. Then the cot began to move back out into the room, and it was over. They removed the IV, and I was free to discard the patient gown, dress in my own clothes again, and be on my way. One test down, but more to go!

Next were the pulmonary function tests. I remember being incredibly irritated with a nice volunteer who said kindly, "I'll take you over to the pulmonary lab in a wheelchair."

"I'm perfectly capable of walking over," I cried. "I don't need a wheelchair!" *After all, I'm walking forty-five minutes a day on the treadmill! Better than she can do*, I thought. That treadmill was my "thinking time," as I recall.

"But most people who have this test done can't make that long walk," she exclaimed. Finally, she reluctantly said, "OK," and I walked from the clinic to the pulmonary lab in the hospital where I inhaled and exhaled into a machine as instructed.

The pleasant technician promptly informed me, "The results of the tests are excellent." Even though I hadn't anticipated any problems with that test, I was relieved to know there was no problem with lung capacity, and I felt incredibly pleased with myself. I had passed the test with flying colors.

That afternoon I had the bronchoscopy, the worst of all the diagnostic experiences. The pulmonologist numbed my throat and gently began to push a tube down through the bronchus into my lung. At first I just kept swallowing, but then I gagged, and it became increasingly painful as he tried to go deeper and deeper, with no success. Finally, my gentle and kind pulmonologist gave up and said, "I'm really sorry, but it is too far down in the lung. We just can't reach it to take a sample for a biopsy. In order to make a diagnosis, we'll have to go in through the chest wall and do a needle biopsy." So there was still no answer, no diagnosis; I remained unsure what my future held. It seemed that there was still a chance that it was something else, but it was time to know what I was dealing with, and in my heart of hearts, I *knew*. It was cancer. *I may as well begin to accept it,* I thought—*just a bit.* But then I would think again, *It could be something else. Could be!*

Again, life went on. We went to Minneapolis to the Guthrie Theater for a play and out to dinner with friends. We saw *The Playboy of the Western World,* and as I read my program before the performance began, I can still remember thinking how much I felt like those theatergoers who first saw this play at the beginning of the century in Dublin. I also wanted to riot, to rebel against the plot—the surprising turn the plot of my life was taking. But, of course, I didn't, and I still said nothing to anyone about what was happening. It was time, though, and we knew it, so we invited Eric, Susie, and Katie for lunch after church the next Sunday.

This was the hardest thing yet, except for initially walking in the apartment door and telling Wayne that I had a mass in my chest. Oh, how I didn't want to tell them what was going on! I just wanted it to go away—but it wasn't going away! I have no idea what we served them, or what we talked about as we sat around the table. All I remember is sitting in my spot at the dining room table and getting up after we finished eating—presumably to go to the bathroom, but really to reapply lipstick so I wouldn't appear pale or sick. Even though I had no cough, I was hypersensitive about coughing, or even clearing my throat. I didn't want to look or sound sick! I felt fine, except for this fear growing inside of me like a monster. I kept talking about trivial things, and I can still vividly hear Wayne say, "Katie, want to go for a walk in the hall?" and the sinking feeling I experienced as she said eagerly, "Sure, Papa!" She always wanted to go for a walk at River Plaza, for she loved it there and knew everyone, including the dogs. She always looked forward to Grandpa giving her a ride on the wheeled chairs in the lounge down the hall. Soon they were on their way out the door. *This is it,* I told myself; *I have to tell Eric and Susie what is going on.* Oh, how I wished that I could have run out the door and joined Katie and Wayne on their walk!

The strange thing is that I have absolutely no recollection of what I said. I think Eric said something like "What's up, Mom?"

And I remember that Susie feared I was going to tell them we were getting a divorce. I assume I reassured them that we were sticking together, and then gave them a summary of symptoms and what had been going on with physician appointments and tests. I know I tried to downplay it and reassured them that we really didn't know what it was yet, but the whole rest of the afternoon is a total blank in my memory. It's just the feelings that stick in my memory. I felt terrible to worry them. There was also the feeling of guilt, for, of course, they both knew that I had smoked, even though I had quit smoking before I ever met Susie. Later that evening we went to a soup supper in our building, and I remember people asking the innocent question, "How are you?" I felt like a liar as I smiled and said, "Fine." But by this point, I was getting good at that.

When I look at the calendar for January of that year, it continues to amaze me, for it was filled with the usual activities. On closer look, however, you can see the addition of things like an appointment with a pulmonologist. When I met with him, his voice was soft-spoken and reassuring but his words were far from encouraging as he said, "In all likelihood it *is* cancer, but we need to schedule a biopsy to confirm the diagnosis. In the meantime, I'd like you to set up appointments with a surgeon and an oncologist who will tell you about a study at Mayo Clinic for people in early stages of lung cancer."

I offered a weak smile, and replied, "OK," as I felt an odd numbness engulf my body. Leaving the office, I could feel the hope that this was something other than cancer draining out of me, like the air slowly going out of a balloon, but the balloon wasn't empty yet. *They still don't know for sure,* I thought, driving aimlessly around before meeting some friends for lunch. I still didn't tell anyone about my potential diagnosis, but knew that I at least needed to tell my friend Sandi. Everyone else could wait until I knew more. I called Sandi and scheduled a lunch for the next week. Ah! I didn't have to tell her—not quite yet! It seemed a big step that I had at least set up a luncheon date.

Then we had another day with Katie. She was incredibly cute and so much fun! I almost could forget about the possibility of cancer when she made me laugh with her funny antics—like making a face and growling at our cat, Mandy, or taking all of the linens out of a chest and spreading them around the room while I thought she was napping. Well, perhaps, that incident didn't make me laugh—until later.

Grandma and Katie

But then there would be the terrible fear again, that I would never live to see her grow up, or get to know her new sister or brother who was going to make an appearance in our lives soon. At this time, Katie's favorite movie in the whole world was *The Lion King*. She could watch it over and over, and the one thing I didn't want to think about right then was the circle of life. She would snuggle up against me as we watched, and I would fight to hold back the tears. The world went on for Simba after the death of Mufasa, and I knew that it would go on for Katie after my death, but I *so* didn't want to die—not now! I wanted to be a part of her life for a long time, and of that of her new sister or brother, who I didn't even know yet.

There was a baby shower for Susie one evening that week. My regular family physician, Sue, who is a good friend of Eric and Susie's, was there. This was the first time I had seen her during this whole experience, which seemed like a lifetime, but in reality had been only two and a half weeks. It seemed like weeks between appointments, but as I look back at the calendar, I can see that the clinic staff was really fantastic at moving me quickly through the system. At some point during the shower, Sue pulled me aside and offered some reassuring words. "Remember, we aren't sure what it is yet, and even if it is cancer, the spot on your lung is very small." Just not hearing the word *mass* made me feel better. A *spot* sounded so much smaller! After that conversation, I actually had fun at the shower. I enjoyed talking with Susie's friends and managed to escape from my fears for a few hours, getting caught up in the excitement of this new grandchild.

We had tickets to another St. Paul Chamber Orchestra concert in the Twin Cities and we stayed with Pat and Heidi again. I vividly remember looking around the concert hall as we sat in the Ordway Theater and noticing a few women who wore pretty scarves wrapped around their heads and several men with clean-shaven heads. I wondered, *Are these simply fashion statements or have they lost their hair to chemotherapy?* I speculated about how many other people sitting there, looking perfectly normal, were waiting for the results of diagnostic tests or battling cancer. This was something I had really never thought about as I looked at a crowd before, and somehow it made me feel not quite so alone. That visit was when I finally told Pat and Heidi what was going on. I didn't want to tell them, but I was holding this huge pain and fear inside of me, and I knew it was time to begin to let it go, to share it with those close to me. Pat was shocked and looked stricken, as I had known he would. It was too close to the time that Jan had died. I tried to hold out to him the little glimmer of hope that I still hung on to, but I don't think I was very convincing, for I, more and more, thought they were going to tell me it was cancer. I remember always wanting to keep my lipstick fresh, lest I look pale or sick, and being overly self-conscious if I had to cough, even if I had just swallowed something wrong. I didn't want to appear sick. I was obsessed with that, and perhaps continued to be so throughout the whole ordeal.

We drove from the Twin Cities to Madeline Island so that we could be at our church for the annual meeting. The president of the council wasn't at the meeting, for his wife had recently been diagnosed with cancer. We didn't know it then, but he was soon to resign his position, and I was going to become much more involved in the business of the church—because of two cancer diagnoses. At that point, I could only wonder what the future held for me. When looking at the semi-annual report for that winter, it is evident that I took on more and more responsibility on the council. There was no president's report, but a report, written by me, from the church council. Not only was our life going on, so was the life of the church, and I was obviously a busy part of it, for my name is signed to a number of the committee reports. I remember working with our pastor on council agendas and writing reports from the council for our church newsletter. In essence, I was taking on the responsibility of council president as well as doing the job of secretary, but in looking back at those reports, you can see no evidence of the fear and sense of foreboding I was experiencing. All of those things helped me during that period, for they gave me a positive focus for my energies—outside of my fear and myself.

But I digress. We headed back to Eau Claire the day after the meeting, after allowing time to take a deep breath and relax one more Sunday afternoon on the island. Tuesday morning we went to see the surgeon. He was very pleasant, and I don't recall having any terrible reaction to the visit, just that it was looking more and more like cancer, *but* it wasn't for sure yet. It still could be something else! The surgeon could just cut it out. I'd had surgery before, and I could deal with it again! As I look at the calendar, I see notes about people whom I needed to call to arrange social events. In my memory, I could think of nothing else at this point, but obviously, I did. We met close friends that night, and I think I still said nothing to them. I didn't know for sure, of course! We just talked about normal things—politics, church, what was going on at the University of Wisconsin–Eau Claire, where Wayne, I, and many of our friends had taught for decades. How I loved to talk about *normal* things! But there were always those times when my mind wandered away, when I thought about what it would be like to be a *cancer* patient.

The appointment I dreaded most was the next morning. It was with the oncologist who would tell us about the study I could opt into if my diagnosis was cancer. Who wants to go to an oncologist when they don't even know if they have cancer?!? As I typed that last sentence, my fingers banged harder than usual on the keys. The appointment was terrible! I sat in the waiting room and looked around at the others there. No one looked like me. No one looked healthy. One woman had a completely bald head and was pale and emaciated. Someone else was jaundiced and had a scarf tied haphazardly around her head. Everyone looked so *sick*! This couldn't be right! I couldn't belong here. Then, after what was probably only a few minutes, but seemed like forever, my name was called. One of my old students was there, and it felt so good to chat normally with someone for a few minutes, but then Wayne and I were in an exam room. As the door closed, I saw the exit sign in the hall disappear. Oh, how I wanted to exit—to run, to escape! Then, this man, who appeared to me at the time like a scrawny little eighteen year old, walked into the room and introduced himself to us. *No, surely, this can't be the physician*, I thought, but yes, it was. He told us about the study and gave us some reading material to take home, but it seemed impossible to trust someone who looked so young. Actually, I quickly grew to like and respect him a great deal, but that day

I couldn't wait to get away from him. In retrospect, I think it would have been virtually impossible to respond positively to any oncologist at that point. I have no idea what to tell an oncologist that would make that situation easier for people, but I really can't think how this could have been worse! One thing I learned was that in order for me to be in the study, my diagnosis would have to be confirmed by lung biopsy, since they were unable to do it with the bronchoscopy. "Also, you will need to have a mediastinoscopy to see if it has spread to the lymph nodes," he explained. "It's just a minor surgical procedure. The surgeon will make a tiny incision and use a scope to look down in your chest and biopsy your lymph nodes." He added, "If it has spread to the nodes, you will not be eligible for the study, for that would mean it is too far advanced." *Too far advanced!* What horrific words. I wasn't even thoroughly convinced that I had cancer. *Surely, it can't be too far advanced!* Some little part of me began to say, *OK, Gay, if this is cancer, give it every shot! Why not be in a Mayo Clinic study?* The tests were scheduled for the next week. A feeling of foreboding crept around me like a fog. In fact, it almost seemed like I was watching this happen in a movie on a blurry TV screen. Surely, this couldn't be me!

The week went on, and we did normal things—enjoying our friends and caring for Katie. To everyone else, to the best of my knowledge, all looked fine with the Lindquists. After a dinner party one evening, I can still remember lying in bed with my back to Wayne. Instead of looking out the window at the trees and the streetlights across the river, I looked at the wall above an antique bachelor's chest, watching the shadows of the branches waving in the breeze outside our window. The tears ran down my cheeks. *Why me?* I asked. *I smoked, but haven't for years. Other people smoked more and longer than I did, and they didn't get lung cancer!* Then I asked myself, *What if I never see Katie grow up?* I tried to stop my racing mind—picturing myself floating on an air mattress on a quiet lake, feeling the warmth of the sun on my body. But I couldn't hold on to that image. The one that surfaced in my mind was Katie in a wedding gown with a tall, handsome young man at her side. Wayne was sitting in a front pew of a church with an empty seat beside him. Then a faceless woman came to join him. *Would I want someone else beside him?* I asked myself. *Of course I would want him to be happy, but...* I petted the purring Mandy, who slept snuggled against my side, drawing comfort from her warmth and the soft vibration of her purring body, and finally floated away into sleep. Other nights I would think about the new grandchild on the way and remember Jan, who had only lived for a year and a half after she was diagnosed. I remembered that she had small-cell carcinoma, and how, naively, when she was first diagnosed, I thought, *That can't be so bad! Small cell must be better than large cell.* But, of course, it's not, for survival statistics are worse for small cell than other types. My mind raced, and sleep eluded me.

On those nights, lying in bed thinking, I realized lung cancer isn't lung cancer isn't lung cancer. It made a big difference what type I had. The oncologist had provided us with statistics, and with some types, if diagnosed early, chances for long-term survival were better than with others, but still not good. It was not good with any of them! Night after night, I lay there silently thinking about my grandchildren and how much I wanted to watch them grow up into strong, healthy, good people. I prayed, not for health, but, *Let Thy will be done,* possibly out of some kind of superstition. Perhaps I was afraid of some kind of retribution for asking too selfish a favor from God. This was not an intellectual thought but some deep, strange, fearful gut feeling. I did, however, ask God for strength to cope with whatever lay ahead, for both my family and me. *Please, dear God, be with them. Help them,* I prayed. As I look back at the whole experience from this vantage point years later, I truly believe that it was those prayers, and God answering those prayers, that gave me the strength and courage to get through it all. God helped me to use my inner resources and brought support in many ways from the people around me.

Finally, the time came that I had to tell Sandi, one of my closest friends and a teaching colleague of many years, what was happening. I hated it! We met for lunch and I asked about what was going on in the School of Nursing and with her family. I stalled and stalled, but knew it was time to tell her. I tried, but the words wouldn't come. Finally I said, "Sandi ... there's something I have to tell you ..." She sat quietly for a few minutes just looking at me. Then she reached across the table and squeezed my hand. Eventually more words came and we could talk about it, but at first there was just silence, tears, and tightly grasped fingers. Again, there was the guilt. I had smoked. She had never smoked, and I could imagine that she could think I should have been smart enough to avoid this. If she had those thoughts, she certainly never shared them with me. Love and support were all I received from her throughout the whole experience. I was aware, when telling her, that she also needed reassurance, and tried to provide it by saying, "It might not be cancer, you know, and if it is, the spot is very small." Spot on your lung sounded so much better than a mass in your chest! Sometimes it was easier to reassure others than myself, but I'm not sure I was always convincing.

February 1998

My birthday, February 2, Groundhog Day. I know that we celebrated my sixtieth birthday with Eric, Susie, and Katie, but nothing is written on the calendar, and I can recall nothing of the day—just remembering that I was sixty years old and had a needle biopsy of my lung scheduled for the next day.

Memories of that next day are foggy as well. To the best of my knowledge, Wayne and I were at the hospital early in the morning, and Eric and Susie arrived shortly after. Surgi-center seemed familiar, for I had supervised senior students there not too many years earlier, and I knew a number of former students and staff there. They were all great and incredibly supportive, but it was still a difficult, frightening experience. How much more horrific this would be to someone who was in a totally strange environment, surrounded by strangers. I really remember nothing about the procedure itself, just being wheeled through a maze of halls on a surgical cart, back into what seemed to be the bowels of the hospital and into a procedure room. I felt a prick, a numb spot on my back, and suddenly I was being rolled back to a room in the surgi-center where my family was waiting. Only strange things stick out in my memory. I remember a painting, done by a friend of ours, hanging on a wall that I was quickly wheeled past. I remember my cart sitting diagonally in the surgi-center room. I wanted to straighten that cart out. It was off kilter, just like all of the rest of my life right then. My family gathered around the cart, and I assured them, "I'm fine. It didn't even hurt." Then the pulmonologist came in the room. I searched his face as he came toward me, and his kind eyes looked directly into mine as he said the words I had been dreading to hear. "I'm sorry. Yes, it is cancer! It's adenocarcinoma." I wasn't sure what that meant in terms of my prognosis yet, but at least I knew that it wasn't small cell, the type that had killed my friend Jan so quickly!

Cancer. *Lung cancer*, I thought as I lay in bed that night watching the shadows of tree limbs move silently on our bedroom wall. Lung cancer *kills* people, people like Jan. My mind played gingerly with thoughts of death. *Am I afraid of death? No*, I thought hesitantly, *not of being dead. I just desperately want to be here. It's the process of dying that I fear!* My mind wandered. *If I die, will I be unable to catch my breath or speak like Uncle Ivan the last time I saw him alive?* I shuddered as I remembered one of the first deaths I had ever seen. I was a young staff nurse on a large, very understaffed gynecological unit. I could still vividly see a young woman clawing at the bed covers and striking out, even hear her agonized cursing of God as she strained for her final breaths. That had been one of the most frightening, powerless moments of my life! No words or actions I offered could bring her comfort. I had absolutely no idea how to help her with that process of dying, no way to help her find any kind of peace. It was truly a living nightmare. Then I tried to comfort myself with thoughts of other deaths—remembering the papery feel of my grandmother's skin as I held her frail wrist until, finally, her pulse slowly faded away as she lay peacefully sleeping, the shadow of a smile on her lips. I recalled my mother's death many years later. She just drifted away, her respirations becoming increasingly irregular as I sat stroking her hand and saying my final thank yous and good-bye. She had even seemed to wait until I had graded my final papers at the end of a semester, as if she were somehow still in control. They had both seemed so at peace. Could I be like that? I hoped so. Then I screamed silently inside my head, *But they were old! They had lived long, full lives. I'm only sixty years old, with a lot of living left to do. I have to fight. To fight this monster growing inside me!* Finally, I fell into a restless sleep filled with dark, shadowy dreams.

Another night I lay there reflecting on my own life. *If I die, how will others look back on my life? How will people remember me?* I recalled my cousin BJ's wake and being overwhelmed by the people who went forward to talk about how she had influenced their lives. A middle-aged man said, "I was in second grade and had outgrown my brother's hand-me-down coat." Then, looking down at her inert body, he tearfully added, "*This* woman gave me a new, warm, blue plaid coat. It was the best gift I ever received!"

An elderly woman who lived down the street from her said, "She made the best blueberry muffins in the whole world," and her voice cracked as she added, "She brought me some the morning after my husband died, and almost every Saturday until she got sick." People poured forward, one after another, telling how she had helped them through difficult times, and challenged or inspired them to achieve more in their lives than they had thought possible. What would people have to say about me? It was too easy to remember the times I had hurried a student out of my office because I needed to get home in time for a dinner party, or made excuses to get off the phone when a colleague called to chat because she was lonely. It was much more difficult to remember the times I had been thoughtful and sensitive to the needs of others.

But now it was real. I couldn't spend all of my time reflecting. I had a diagnosis and it was time to begin telling close friends what was going on. That was so hard! Each time I told someone I would feel a brief sense of relief, but then there would be the next person I should tell, and it felt a little like picking a scab off a cut. It would start bleeding again. Moreover, each time I had to feel guilty—especially with my non-smoking friends, although most of us had smoked in the old days. In retrospect, I'm sure it aroused fear in each of them. They were concerned about me, but those former smokers must have had fears for themselves as well. It seemed necessary to offer reassurance to each person. I was a nurse, after all. I was supposed to be the comforter, not the one to cause the pain. This came naturally, but at times, it was difficult, and sometimes it seemed an additional burden, one that was hard to bear.

A few days later, I had the next procedure, a mediastinoscopy. This was what would tell me if cancer had spread to my lymph nodes. I knew the mass was small and I just couldn't believe that it might have spread to my lymph nodes. But then again, a few weeks earlier, I couldn't have believed it could be cancer! Anyway, by now I felt quite at home at the surgi-center, and once again had people I knew around me to provide me with support. I can't describe how much that meant to me. But this wasn't like the other tests. This was done on a Friday morning and my appointment with the surgeon, when I would get the results, wasn't scheduled until Tuesday morning. I have often remembered that weekend while watching the film, *That's Life*, one of our old favorites. As Julie Andrews awaits the results of her biopsy, I want to strangle members of her family who are so self-centered and insensitive. She has to be the one who comforts everyone else. Fortunately, my family was not like hers, but still, the waiting was incredibly difficult.

Finally, Tuesday morning arrived. Wayne and I sat silently, side by side, in the exam room, and I picked up a magazine, but my eyes scanned the contents of the room rather than looking at the pages in front of me. "Your lymph nodes are completely *clean!*" the surgeon exclaimed as he walked in the door. That was the first good news I had received in this whole saga. My face must have shown my great relief, for he looked surprised and asked, "Are you relieved?"

My response was just a simple, "Of course!" but I remember feeling incredulous at his response. Of course I was relieved! My chances of survival had just increased—at least a bit. My chances of an early death were, hopefully, less. I had a lunch scheduled for that day, and thank goodness, it could be a celebration. I'm not sure how I would have handled it if I had just learned that the cancer had spread to my lymph nodes.

Again, my calendar shows normal activities. The week was filled with babysitting and visits with friends. Two couples came from out of town, and I remember wondering, *Do they think this will be the last time they ever see me looking normal?* That, of course, remains unknown, but I do recall that most of our friends were extremely sensitive and caring. Many people experience friends kind of dropping them at this point, but that wasn't what I encountered, with the exception of one former colleague who never contacted me. A number of the cards and phone calls I received were from people who said she had told them about my diagnosis, so I knew she was aware of what I was going through, and I must admit it was a bit hurtful not to hear from her. One other friend stands out in my mind because of her response, or lack thereof. I certainly didn't want a big deal made out of it, but I was puzzled, as was Wayne, for she made an offhand comment saying it was too bad but quickly went on to talk about her kids and all the things going on in her life. It was as if I had a hangnail. "This is no hangnail! It is lung cancer!" I wanted to scream at her but, of course, I did no such thing. Who knows how one should react to a friend's sharing of this type of diagnosis? Sometimes it is very difficult to know what to say. I'm sure I have not always responded as a friend might have wished I had, but this whole experience certainly helped me to try to be more sensitive to what friends are experiencing. Overall, I was amazed and pleased at the number of people from whom I received cards, visits, or phone calls. They all meant a great deal to me.

Next was the appointment with the oncologist. I liked him more this time. I suppose that was partly because I had at least begun to accept the fact that I had cancer. I could at least say the word, in relation to myself, out loud at this point. That, in and of itself, was a big step. After a lot of thought, Wayne and I decided that I should be a part of the Mayo Clinic study. This meant I would go through chemotherapy before surgery. Perhaps it doesn't sound like it should be a major concern, whether surgery or chemotherapy comes first, but once I began to accept that I did have cancer, my gut response was that I wanted it *gone*. I wanted it cut out of me as soon as possible, just like my offending uterus when fibroids were making life unbearable. But, on the other hand, some studies showed better survival rates for people who had chemotherapy prior to surgery, so I decided to go that route. It was set. Lab tests were done. Another X-ray was taken, and my first round of chemotherapy was scheduled.

Wayside # 1

The first stop for a moment of reflection is on a pedestrian bridge over the Chippewa River—one of my old favorite "thinking spots." Snow, once pure and white, but now covered with black dirt and grime, is piled along the walk approaching the bridge. Ice lines the shores, and portions of the river are frozen over, making it look cold and forbidding. Yet there is a frigid beauty in the ice formations along the shore and the snow hanging on the trees. Far below the bridge, a strong current keeps a portion of the river open. That constant flowing of the river has always intrigued me, for it's so different from the endless waves hitting the shore of Lake Superior or the Gulf of Mexico. It's always moving forward, symbolizing to me, especially during this period of my life, the sense of life going on—life that I so much wanted to be a part of. I hoped that I had a long way to go before I reached the sea.

What did I think about as I looked down from that bridge? Looking back now, what did I learn that might be helpful to others? I must acknowledge that, as difficult as this encounter with cancer was, many people have experiences far more difficult. A number of things beyond my control made my journey much easier than it is for many. First of all, my family and friends were incredibly supportive, and I know this is not true for everyone. Some people have to face such situations feeling isolated and alone, which must make it even more challenging. Secondly, my familiarity with the health care system and knowing many of the care providers made it easier, but of course being the patient is an entirely different experience from being the care provider. Often having former students as care providers made me feel proud, as I observed what fine nurses they had become, but it also increased my need to appear brave and strong, which often was a challenge and, at times, downright difficult. One other major factor, of course, that eased my journey was the fact that I felt well and wasn't dealing with physical pain or discomfort. Trying to manage physical pain can only increase the difficulty of coping with the emotional pain associated with a cancer diagnosis.

I did, however, have control over some of the things happening in my life during that diagnostic period, and perhaps that is where the lessons lie. One thing was keeping actively involved in life, like that rapidly moving current in the river, and not allowing myself to become totally overwhelmed by what was happening to me. I tried to stay physically, mentally, spiritually, and socially active. A variety of things, of course, influence a person's ability to do this, such as whether you are employed or retired, whether or not you are dealing with physical pain, your religious beliefs, and your social support group. I used the treadmill most days and went for frequent walks, for I wanted to be in the best physical condition possible for my chemotherapy and impending surgery. These walks provided excellent thinking time as well as physical conditioning. Both Wayne and I did things with our family, caring for Katie and shopping for the soon-to-arrive grandchild. We continued to entertain and we went out with friends. We also went as often as possible to our island home where we can find a peace that seems more accessible to us than it is elsewhere. I was retired, so I didn't have a job to keep my mind active but I was very involved in my volunteer activities, especially at our church. My experiences there helped me spiritually, but also my increasing responsibilities helped to keep me intellectually active—working on budgets, writing reports, and planning for meetings. This doesn't mean that there wasn't plenty of time for introspection, and even fear and grieving at times, but they didn't consume my life.

Looking back, I can see how important it was to balance the time spent being actively involved in life with the time for introspection and reflection. They are both necessary. Like the frozen edges of the river, I needed rest in order to gain strength for the strong currents of what was to come. The diagnosis of cancer, especially a type with a guarded prognosis, forces you to face the possibility of death, and in order to do this I believe it is essential to consider life. What is important to you? What are your priorities as you face the future— whatever that future might hold? It seems unfortunate that often we become so involved in the busy-ness of everyday life that we don't take time to really think about what is important to us. It would be a shame to pass up this opportunity to do just that! Too many times in the past, my job or doing work around the house took priority over spending time with valued family and friends. Since my cancer diagnosis, I have made a real effort to put the important people in my life first, but I find that it is something that I, and probably most of us, continually have to work on as we journey through life. It's far too easy to fall back into old patterns.

Another incredibly important thing that helped me though this period was that I was able to reach out for help and support. I wasn't really ready to reach out to other people very much at this point, but I reached out to God. I prayed—at night, as I lay in bed unable to sleep, as I walked, looking off our balcony onto the river, on the island, looking out at Lake Superior. Everywhere. I didn't ask to be cured, but for strength to face what lay ahead and strength for my family. Everyone's beliefs are different, and probably my concept of God now has evolved from what it was then, but most of us believe in some power beyond ourselves. I would encourage everyone to reach out to whatever that is for strength. Whether the strength actually comes from beyond, from those around us, or from within ourselves is irrelevant. The fact is that most of us need a good dose of extra strength as we face the big C word, so seek it from whatever works for you.

In a way, this experience was a sort of wake-up call, reminding me of my mortality. I took more time just to look at the lake and the river, to watch the snowflakes fall, to savor the smell of a crackling fire or chili simmering on the stove, and to snuggle with my granddaughter—just to enjoy the everyday things in life. There was something about feeling unsure of how much time I would have on this earth that heightened my senses, making me more acutely aware of the little things in the world around me.

There are also things to be learned from my experiences for family and friends of people going through the diagnosis of cancer. Of course, your loved ones need to talk, but I don't think any of us who have gone through this experience want to talk to everyone about our diagnosis or to talk about it all of the time. Let them know you care and that you are willing to listen, but don't push. Friends who tried to push me to talk about my feelings sometimes made me feel resentful. On the other hand, don't gloss over it as if it were nothing. That can cause resentment as well. Sometimes it may seem difficult to strike the right note. You may feel frustrated, even angry or resentful, that you can't seem to do things right and that all these problems are being heaped upon you. That's OK. It's normal. Remember that you also need support and to talk it through, for your life is forever altered as well.

I often thought of my family and friends as I looked down at the bank surrounding and supporting the raging river. Sometimes it looked dark and grimy, almost tired. As that shoreline needed a blanket of fresh, white snow to brighten and strengthen it, so did my family and friends need a blanket of comfort and support around them, as do all of you who are caring for loved ones dealing with the diagnosis of cancer. Talk to each other about what you are thinking and feeling. Reach out to friends. Sometimes our friends are so busy trying to be supportive to the person with cancer that the family members get forgotten. I know that I got more cards, hugs, and words of encouragement than Wayne did, and he needed them as well.

Reach out to God, or whatever Supreme Being you believe in, if that is helpful to you. You, also, need strength. It's important that you stay involved in life too, not letting the cancer diagnosis consume you. Remember to take time to do some "normal" things when you can. Sometimes just watching a football game or going to a concert or a movie with friends can do wonders for your spirit.

CHAPTER THREE

Beginnings

February–May 1998

I had no idea what to expect. I had heard such horror stories about chemotherapy. People being so sick—nauseated, lying on the bathroom floor, head hanging over the toilet bowl vomiting. Emaciated, weak, frail, dependent. I dreaded it! My oncologist and the wonderful oncology nurse who had once been my student, however, assured me that they would give me medication that would reduce, if not eliminate, the nausea. Having always battled to keep my weight down, I remember thinking that the one good thing that might come out of all of this, if I did have problems with nausea and loss of appetite, was that I might lose weight. They were right about the nausea, however, for I didn't have problems with that, and thus, of course, never had the pleasure of weight loss either, but that was fine with me.

The nurses told me one thing, though, that I really didn't want to hear. I *would*, not *might*, lose my hair. I made an appointment to get my hair cut short so that when it fell out it wouldn't be such a drastic change. I've rarely, if ever, asked anyone to take my picture, but one day when we were taking pictures of Katie, I asked Wayne, "Would you take my picture, too … while I still have hair?"

"Sure," he said with a hesitant smile. That is the picture I'm looking at now. I look happy. Smiling. My hair is long and brown, brushing my shoulders, for I had just let it grow out for the first time in several years. I was standing on the balcony of our apartment at River Plaza with the river in the background, showing the bridge I was walking across when I first coughed up blood. I was wearing jeans, but had put on a pretty ivory silk blouse, a green blazer, and my necklace made from our mothers' wedding and engagement rings for the picture.

Gay at River Plaza

I must have been focused on hair that day, for one of the pictures I took was of Katie, laughing and looking at herself in the mirror, wearing an old wig from the dress-up box.

Katie with wig and high heels

I went to see my hairdresser of many years and faced the painful task of explaining why I wanted my hair cut short. She was great! After her initial shock and expression of sorrow, she told me a number of stories about clients of hers who have had their hair come back in curly, blonde, or somehow different from what it had been. *Curly hair and no more permanents,* I thought, *now there's a positive thing to look forward to!*

Then the day of my first chemotherapy treatment arrived. Wayne wanted to go with me, and I assured him, "I'll be fine! I don't need you to come with me."

"No, I'm going with you," he insisted. Perhaps that first time, at least, that was OK with me, for, of course, I really had no idea what to expect. Once again, my former student was there, and she was the one who easily slipped the IV needle into my vein. All of the nurses were great about telling me each thing they were doing, what each medication was, and how it would make me feel. I sat in a comfortable recliner watching the drip … drip … drip … of the IV hanging above my head, thinking of the description you often hear of chemo—poison. *Will its poison kill the insidious cells invading my lung?* I mused. *What else will it do to my body? How will it make me feel?* But I felt nothing, until suddenly there was the intense flushing feeling they had forewarned me about. The feeling passed, the drip continued, and finally I could begin to relax a bit. Wayne and I watched some news on CNN, talked a little, and then I sent him off to lunch. I sat there quietly, glad that treatment had begun, and read the book I had brought along. Then, surprisingly soon, it was over, the nurse discontinued my IV, and told me I could go. I was pleasantly surprised that I really felt no adverse effects at all. No nausea. No vomiting. Nothing! Whew! One down. Two to go. Three rounds of chemotherapy. That was all I was going to have. I thought I had it made. I felt great!

Three days later, I developed terrible pains in my legs. I knew it must have metastasized to the bone. What else could cause such pain? *Oh, dear God,* I thought. *How am I going to get through this?*

I remembered stories I had heard and a novel I had read that all too vividly described the excruciating pain that can be associated with bone cancer. Then, about twenty-four hours later, the pain was gone! Completely! Relieved, I thought, *Perhaps it wasn't bone cancer after all.* Eventually, I learned that sometimes that kind of deep bone pain occurs when the chemotherapeutic agents are working on the bone marrow. But then a chain of events started that made me think much less about myself for a while.

We were scheduled to go to a leadership retreat in Duluth, Minnesota, for our church on Madeline Island, and I was pleased that I felt so well, for I hadn't been sure I would feel like going. Being involved in discussion of plans for the future seemed like an especially positive thing to be doing right then. We were getting things organized to leave when the phone rang, and suddenly I heard my cousin John's voice in my ear. "Mom died this morning, Gay. The funeral will be Tuesday."

"Oh, John," I replied, "I'm so sorry!" while quickly realizing, *That's in the middle of the retreat.* I don't get back to Iowa, where I grew up, often, and I had been very fond of my aunt and her sons as I was growing up, so I quickly said, "We'll be there!" So we headed south, back to Iowa, the land of my childhood, instead of to Duluth to plan for the future.

We had always told our son and daughter-in-law where we would be staying when we were on a trip, but this time we would only be sleeping overnight in a motel. We would go to the funeral and return home that afternoon. This was before the time when we all joined the convenient world of cell phones.

The evening before the service, we were at the funeral home visiting with relatives that I hadn't seen for several years. It was a sad time, but also joyful, for we were reuniting and enjoying reminiscing. It was, though, made a little more difficult by having to explain to everyone about my cancer, for I had not yet told any of my relatives about it. I was deep in conversation with someone when one of my cousins came over to me and said, "There's a phone call for you in the funeral home office, Gay." I felt momentarily disoriented. *Who could possibly know where I am except for the other people here?* I asked myself. It always sounds strange to hear someone say that their heart is pounding, but I literally felt it banging in my chest, and my hands were shaking as I picked up the phone. Then I heard the voice of Eric on the other end of the line—our clever son who had thought to call the police in this small Iowa town to track us down. For a moment, I couldn't really process what he was saying. Susie's pregnancy had gone perfectly with Katie. Everything had been the same this time. She was due in four weeks. Everything was fine. It had to be fine! But that wasn't what Eric was saying on the other end of the line. "Susie went in for a routine prenatal visit, and they did one last sonogram. It shows that the baby has a possible heart defect, Mom." I have no recollection of what I said next, but I remember him saying, "We're driving to Minneapolis, so when the baby is born it will be at Minneapolis Children's Hospital. There will be pediatric cardiologists right there." *No,* I thought! *This can't be happening!* But it was. "Don't drive tonight!" he said. "Come in the morning." Reluctantly, we agreed, said our good-byes to my Iowa relatives and went back to our motel room. Just after we arrived, the phone rang. "Susie's water broke," Eric said. "They're taking her to Minneapolis in an ambulance, and I'm driving up. Our friend, Judy, is coming over to spend the night with Katie and take her to day care in the morning." Before he hung up, he repeated, "Don't drive tonight. Come in the morning."

Later we lay side by side at the motel, occasionally clasping hands, saying little, and sleeping even less. Finally, when the clock said four o'clock, the phone rang. "You have a grandson!" Eric declared. Actually, I don't remember how much we learned at that point about the baby's heart defects, just that we quickly headed north on Interstate 35, watching the crimson sun rise over the frozen Iowa fields. How many emergencies had I responded to—driving on I-35, not knowing what I would find when I reached my parents' home? More than I care to remember—but this was different. I was driving north toward a new grandchild who had not even had a chance at life yet, not south toward aging parents who had lived long, full lives. We were silent, and my tears flowed freely as we drove.

We found a spot to park in the unfamiliar parking garage and somehow quickly found Eric. Our beautiful daughter-in-law, Susie, had tears streaming down her cheeks when we approached her bed. To this day, I can hear her crying, "We must never go away again and not know how to reach each other!" Only recently, and long after we all started carrying cell phones, have I stopped writing out a complete itinerary for her when we go on a trip. We held each other, and cried as Eric and Susie told us that our grandson had five heart defects, tetralogy of Fallot, and the absence of a pulmonary valve. I found it difficult to absorb what they were saying as I listened to their words, picturing the blue-tinged, sickly infants I had seen many years ago as a young nurse. Then Eric helped Susie into a wheelchair, and we all went to see Jackson Arthur Lindquist. This name brought tears of joy, for Arthur had been the name of both of our fathers and is Eric's middle name, but it was such a big name for such a tiny boy! Here he was, this eagerly awaited grandchild, in the neonatal ICU, attached to a myriad of tubes and wires.

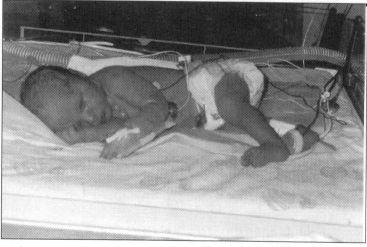

Jackson in Neonatal ICU

Years ago, I had been head nurse in a newborn nursery, and had worked in neonatal ICU, so it shouldn't have been overwhelming, and hopefully I was reassuring to my son and daughter-in-law. Still, it was a jolt to see his tiny body lying there looking so incredibly fragile. This wasn't just any baby; it was my grandson! I did find comfort, though, in the fact that he was pink—his skin and even his fingernails. I had thought he would look sicker, but he looked perfect. Tiny, but perfect. Only the machinery he was attached to suggested the severity of his problems.

We learned more about his diagnosis from the nurses and physician. Five heart defects sounds overwhelming, but actually it was the absence of the pulmonary valve that helped his little body compensate for the defects in tetralogy of Fallot. The fact that he looked so healthy made it easier for me to reassure Eric and Susie. Also, it was comforting to all of us that his cardiologist was the daughter of dear friends on Madeline Island. But still, five heart defects! That was overwhelming. But hold together I did. At least that is my memory. I automatically tried to slip into the role of mother/nurse, offering whatever comfort I could; in fact, I didn't even think about myself or my cancer diagnosis for a while. But we couldn't stay long, for we needed to drive back to Eau Claire to pick up Katie at day care.

I was fine until we got out to the parking garage, where I suddenly burst into uncontrollable sobbing. I knew I should be reassuring Wayne, but instead I was frightening him more. "Is it worse than I think?" he asked. I couldn't answer. I could only picture babies and small children with this kind of heart defect many years ago when I started out in nursing. Blue babies, we called them. Then, toddlers who were tiny, with clubbed fingers because of inadequate oxygen, and if they lived that long—preschoolers, squatting, pale and blue, trying to catch their breath, unable to keep up with the other children. This wasn't the grandchild we were supposed to have! How could this be happening?

Finally, I gathered myself together. We wandered through the parking garage looking for our car, having absolutely no recollection of where we had parked it. After walking up and down most of the levels of the garage, we found our car and started toward Eau Claire. Finally, about half way between Minneapolis and Eau Claire, I was able to talk to Wayne about my hysterical episode, to explain what kind of future babies with tetralogy of Fallot had when I started out in nursing and how much things have improved. They couldn't do surgery until they were school age then. Now they do it in infancy, before they develop the terrible complications they once had. I don't know if these words helped, but they were the only words that I had.

Then we were at the day care center to pick up Katie. We were to collect her, care for her, and love her, but we also had to explain to this beautiful little three-and-a-half-year old girl about her new little brother and his heart defects. It's difficult to remember exactly how we did that, but I think my pediatric nursing and grandparenting experiences somehow miraculously combined to help me with the job—with a lot of help from God. We were incredibly thankful that she was so used to being with us and so comfortable with us. She seemed to trust us and believed my words when I told her they could fix her little brother's heart.

Now this is strange, for the memories have flowed so freely up until this point, and here there seems to be a blank, with just a few individual scenes appearing through the haze. One is walking into the neonatal ICU the next day with Katie, totally forgetting myself and my cancer. I focused only on explaining the tubes and wires connected to her new brother and helping to rearrange all those life-saving connections as she sat in a rocking chair and held her brother, Jackson, in her arms for the first time. She was such a brave little girl, and I remember feeling enormous pride in her.

It seemed an amazingly short time before Jackson was gradually disconnected from his tubes and allowed to go home. I can still see him arriving home, looking surprisingly healthy in his forest green velour hooded suit, sleeping in his car seat.

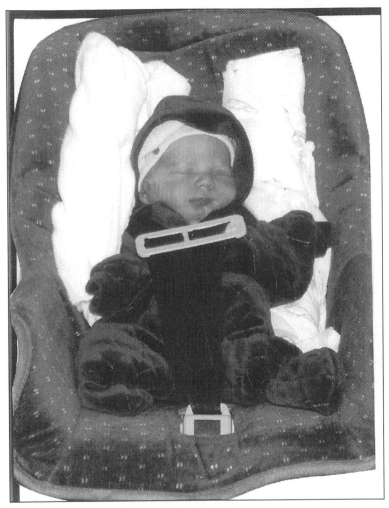

Jackson at home

What a miracle he was! But then we didn't know how truly miraculous he would turn out to be. We were moving forward, both Jackson and I, on our journeys. This intense fight for life, I believe, helped to establish a special bond between us.

CHAPTER FOUR

Hair

March–May 1998

One of my vivid memories is a cold, blustery March afternoon when I walked into Kathy's Wig Shop, tightly holding onto Wayne's hand. The nurses had told me I would lose my hair, and I had thought long and hard about whether or not to get a wig. I admired people who exposed their bald beauty proudly to the world and those who wore beautiful, exotic scarves wrapped around their heads. In fact, it made me smile to recall my cousin B.J. and the crazy hats she wore as she bravely battled brain cancer, a fight we had known, even from the beginning, was impossible to win. I just couldn't be one of those brave people. I desperately didn't want to be seen as *sick*. My family and friends all knew what I was dealing with, but I just couldn't advertise it to the world. I wanted to go on with my life in as normal a fashion as possible, to be seen as *normal* to those around me. The kind woman in the wig shop suggested that I try something drastically different from my natural hair. "Why not try being a blonde or a redhead?" she suggested. "Have a little fun!" I tried on cute blonde curls and smooth auburn waves, but my desire to look *normal* prevailed. I ordered one that matched my hair color and new short style as closely as possible. *Maybe later I'll have the nerve to try something a little more daring*, I thought, *but not now.*

Hair. Why was that such an issue for me? It seems that when you're thinking about life and death, hair loss should be very insignificant, but it wasn't for me. About two weeks after starting chemotherapy I began to notice more than the usual amount of hair in my hairbrush. Then one morning I suddenly felt sick as I looked at the hair scattered on my pillow. My hair has always been very thick, so I tried to reassure myself that I could lose quite a bit before it would begin to appear thin. *Maybe it won't really all fall out*, I thought! But soon when I ran my fingers through my hair they would come away full of hair. No, I had to admit it was going to go. I suppose this was so difficult because it was such a visible sign of my cancer. Otherwise, there was nothing anyone could see outwardly that would "give me away."

The Friday before my second chemotherapy treatment we went to the island for a church council meeting. When packing my clothes I reluctantly included the new wig, for by this time my hair was getting very thin. When we got up Saturday morning I was aghast when I looked down at my pillow. There was literally a pile of hair. I reached up to my head and more fell out in my hand. When I looked in the mirror, I saw only patches of sparse hair scattered around my head. My eyes filled with tears. It *looked* like I had cancer! It was real! I felt ugly—and pitiful. I gave in to my sorrow and cried, all the time thinking, *This is silly, hair isn't that important.* Then I closed my eyes, took a deep breath, pulled out my wig and looked at it for a moment. I adjusted it on my head, carefully pulled out a few remaining strands of hair along the hairline and combed them over the wig, trying to make it look as natural as possible. I applied some makeup, looked in the mirror and felt "human" again. Ready, or at least almost ready, to face the world. Questions raced through my mind. *What will people say? Will everyone notice? Does it look natural enough? Will they notice but be too polite to say anything?* Then it was time for my first big outing with the new wig, and I was off to the meeting.

Everyone, of course, asked how I was feeling, and I assured them, "I feel just fine!" while wondering if they all noticed the wig. No one said a word about it. I stayed after the others left to talk to Marina. "My hair is almost gone," I said. "This is the first day I had to wear a wig. Do you think everyone noticed, but just didn't say anything?"

"It looks great!" she said, giving me a hug. "*I* didn't even notice. I'm sure no one else did." It was amazing how much better those few words made me feel.

One morning the next week I looked in the mirror, before my shower, at my nearly bald head. Scraggly strands of hair stuck out in irregular spots on my head. *What good is this amount of hair?* I asked myself, and called to Wayne. "Could you please do me a favor and … shave my head?"

I have no idea how he felt about doing it, but he came to the door, looked at me, and hesitantly said, "I guess. If you're *positive* that's what you want me to do." Then he brought in a chair for me, and we were both absolutely silent as he proceeded to shave my head clean, leaving just a little hair around the front to pull out over the edge of the wig.

After he left the bathroom I looked in the mirror. I didn't recognize the totally bald person who stared back at me. This was a cancer patient! Ugly! Frightening, somehow! I went in the shower, and my tears began to mix with the water—flowing quietly and slowly at first, but eventually pouring out as I became totally overcome by grief. Huge, racking sobs began to shake my body. I sobbed and sobbed and sobbed. I knew Wayne could hear. I suspect he may have been crying as well, but I couldn't stop. These tears, I suspect, were not for my hair alone but were the result of a final acknowledgement that it was real. I had cancer, the disease we all dread. There was no pretending. No denying. It was real. My tears were also for my grandson, that tiny baby with all those defects in his little heart, for our son, our daughter-in-law, and our granddaughter. For Wayne, for all of us. For our *charmed* life that was no more. We all had to face our problems and our mortality, even that of the tiny new baby in our lives. The hot water washed over my body and my bald head for a long time, and then I began to calm myself. Finally, I stopped crying and got out of the shower, but I kept my eyes averted from the mirror. Quickly I dressed, put on my wig, and added some bright lipstick. Then I could look in the mirror. Once again I could recognize the person that looked back at me. It was Gay Joan Seversike Lindquist. Still me!

Katie knew my hair had fallen out and that I was wearing a wig, but she had never seen me without it. One day, as she was playing with things in the dress-up box, she looked at herself in the mirror with a short, curly wig covering her long, straight hair and her curiosity got the best of her. "Take your wig off!" she demanded. "I want to see what you look like without your hair." "Are you sure?" I asked. "It's not very pretty."

"Take it off!" she demanded with a sly smile. I didn't want to frighten her, but I thought I should be natural and honest about it, so I reluctantly pulled it off. She tilted her head, looked at me quizzically for a moment and said, "You can put it back on now. You look better with it!" And that was all there was to it. Later, our son told me that he heard her telling one of her friends, "My grandma lost all of her hair because of the strong medicine she is taking, but it's OK. It will make her better and her hair will all grow back again!" If only I could have accepted it that simply!

I didn't even like to look at my bald head at night. Besides, it got cold! I ordered a soft little sleep cap that I put on each night after I took my wig off, just before we went to bed. I even hated to watch shampoo commercials on television with all those women with long gorgeous hair. It seemed as if the majority of the commercials were for hair products. There were so many of them! As I look back at all of that, I think I probably was a bit fanatical about the whole hair issue. I know some people find wigs uncomfortable, but I was fortunate. Mine was very comfortable and provided me with a lot of solace. It helped to make my journey easier. I still admire those who go with only hats or scarves, but I would probably wear a wig if I ever had to face that situation again.

Shaving my head and the subsequent tears, I suppose, were some kind of turning point. Even though acceptance of this kind of diagnosis never comes all at one time, but in stages, probably with a lot of regression involved, at this point I began more fully to accept what was happening to me. This was necessary before I could begin to move forward and cope with treatment. It's not that I never cried again, for sometimes the tears came unbidden, late at night, as I thought about the possibility of my grandchildren growing up not knowing who I was, as I had never known my father's parents. I'd never really thought much about them because they both had died years before I was born. Suddenly I wondered what kind of people they had been. I knew my grandfather had come from Norway as a young man, and that my grandmother was born as her family crossed Illinois in a covered wagon, but *who* were they? What had been their dreams and aspirations? What had they loved? The thought of my grandchildren never really knowing me was one that I often had to push to the back of my mind during those months of treatment. It was also the thought that often gave me the courage and motivation to fight.

CHAPTER FIVE

Support

February–May 1998

As I look at the calendar for the next two months, I can see that everything seemed to fall into a pattern. Weekly blood tests, lunches or dinners with friends, concerts, returning books to the library. A St. Patrick's Day party, a meeting with our stockbroker. A few days away to the island. Chemotherapy every three weeks, followed by leg pain. It looks like a *normal* life. If it weren't for the places that say *lab* or *chemo*, you could never tell what we were going through.

Unfortunately, my original journal is lost forever, so of course I have no day-to- day record of what I was feeling at that time, but certain things stand out in my memory. I was one of the fortunate ones. I didn't have to suffer problems with nausea, vomiting, or diarrhea, and I was thankful for that, except that I also never experienced the weight loss that I originally had thought might be one of the only benefits of the whole ordeal. I did, though, have problems with constipation. I can remember wondering if it was in my colon as well and if that was a sign of a developing bowel obstruction. Thank goodness for the little book *No More Bad Hair Days* that someone gave me! Since that time, I have given the book as a gift to a number of people going through chemotherapy. It combines common sense advice with humor, a wonderful combination for a difficult time in life. One of its wise sayings is, "There are not enough prunes in the world to cope with chemotherapy!" How reassuring those words were! Perhaps there was no bowel obstruction after all.

The worst side effect I experienced was the leg pain after treatments, but once I figured out the pattern, it was fairly simple to manage. It always occurred on the third day after a treatment, and when I felt the first twinge of discomfort, I would take some over-the-counter pain pills and keep taking them for twenty-four hours or so, always trying to "keep ahead of the pain." I have always preferred showers to baths, but I found that soaking in a warm bath also was helpful. The good thing was that after the first time I learned that the pain would disappear after twenty-four hours or so. This made coping much easier.

One of the things that everyone going through chemotherapy has to be concerned about is the white blood count and the body's ability to fight off infection. This was winter in Wisconsin, and we were frequently caring for a preschooler who attended day care on the weekdays she wasn't with us. She, and frequently many of our friends, had colds. Both Wayne and I were extremely careful about hand washing and trying to stay away, as much as possible, from people with respiratory infections. Once again, I was lucky. Somehow I managed to avoid getting a cold. One time, though, I recall going in for my routine blood work, and because my blood counts were not adequate, my treatment had to be delayed. It made no logical sense, but somehow that made me feel that I had flunked a test. Everything had gone smoothly until then, but now I didn't measure up. Fortunately, a week later, it was fine and I was able to proceed with the treatments.

Fatigue was another issue, although I must have been fortunate here, too, for, at least in my recollections, it wasn't very severe. For the most part I felt like being active and busy all the time, doing the things that I always did. I do recall, however, that, even though I had never really been one to enjoy naps, on the days we babysat for Katie I eagerly looked forward to her nap time, so that I could take one, too. The combination of chemotherapy and a small child can be tiring, but the joy this preschooler brought to my life certainly made chemotherapy more palatable. I couldn't worry about cancer and chemotherapy while listening to Katie's squeals of delight as I pushed her high on a swing or watched her impish grin as she pushed Eric toward the door when he dropped her off at our apartment in the morning, saying, "Go to work, Daddy. Papa needs to fix my eggies!"

I remember other specific things as well—like going to Minneapolis with Susie to take Jack for his first checkup with Allison, his cardiologist. The reassuring pictures on the bulletin board in the waiting room of children with heart defects—growing up, leading active and healthy lives. Watching the beating of his heart on a monitor screen. Dr. Allison's reassurance that he was doing well and that all of the defects could be repaired in one surgery in a few months. How good to know just how much things had changed from the time I was in nursing school many years ago!

Then there was Easter dinner at our apartment. I fixed the table with a damask cloth, carefully hung miniature eggs on our Easter egg tree, put colorful candles in my mom's old crystal candle holders, tied the napkins with matching satin ribbons, arranged tiny flowers in little crystal vases, and filled miniature Easter baskets to set at each place. I wanted it to seem festive, just like a normal holiday. How I hoped that I would be able to fix holiday tables for our family for many years to come! But I wasn't sure. That fear was always there—not too far beneath the surface.

Wayne was my primary support person through this all. He was always there—ready to listen, or just to hold me in his arms. I felt fine physically, and he let me be as independent as I wanted to be, except for going to chemotherapy treatments. That was a different story. He always insisted on going with me, and even though I didn't feel it was necessary, it was nice to know how much he cared. As I look back now, I realize that perhaps this was important to him as well. There was nothing he could do about what was happening, but this was a way for him to be an active part of my treatment. After each treatment, he greeted me with a single gorgeous rose. What a lovely thought! I'm not sure he ever truly realized how much those roses meant to me. I was grateful for all of the support I received, but I was also concerned for Wayne, for it didn't seem that he received that same degree of support, and it was frightening and painful for him, too. I've given that a lot of thought since then. Is this a male/female thing? Do women reach out more to support other women than men do to men? I really don't know. I suspect that may be the case, but I do know that he was left out a bit. I tried to be supportive, but I'm not really sure how effective I was.

Our son, Eric, and daughter-in-law, Susie, were also fantastic, even though they were struggling with their own problems related to Jack's health. They were both there for me, every step of the way. They gave me a tiny guardian angel pin during this time—just a little thing, but it meant so much. I still cherish it. Even recently I had a moment of panic when I couldn't find it in my jewelry box. I don't actually wear it that often, and they may not even know that it's important to me, but I still see it as my own special guardian angel.

And grandchildren! How can you say enough about how the smiles, giggles, and cuddles of a three-and-a-half year old granddaughter help you through the difficult days? I remember all of those happy times with Katie, and then I look at the pictures of Jack. He was so tiny, so cute and full of promise. Those two darling grandchildren encouraged me to fight. I wrote letters to each of them soon after they were born—letters that I will give to them when they're a little older. I see that I closed my letter to Jack by saying, "For my part, I plan to stay around for a long time. After all, I have to watch you grow up!" They were both a major source of my hope and motivation to beat the odds.

Katie, Grandma Gay, and Jackson on Madeline Island

So many people did kind and thoughtful things for me during this time. People called to take me out to lunch. An old friend that I rarely saw called and offered to drive me to chemotherapy or to do anything that would be helpful. She almost sounded disappointed that I didn't really *need* anything, except, perhaps, just to know that she cared. Friends and relatives who had experienced cancer called to reassure me that they were doing well. Other friends, in Arizona for the winter, called regularly just to see how I was doing. One of our neighbors brought me a little plant. Cards arrived, almost daily, from someone, some that I even came to recognize by their distinctive envelopes that made me smile before I even opened them. People did so many thoughtful things! I was overwhelmed by it all. These acts of kindness and support were so helpful to me that I try to use them now as a model for my own life when I hear of others experiencing difficult times.

Another memory of this time is *the look*. It's difficult to describe, but it was the look I got after I responded to the question, "What kind of cancer is it?" There was always the

"Oh," accompanied by an expression that seemed to include pity, lack of hope, and sorrow. Sometimes the questioners' eyes drifted away at that point. Usually *the look* was followed by silence, for no one seemed able to find the right words. After all these years I still get a similar look, but now it's usually followed by a surprised look and, "How long ago did you say that was?" People often still seem a bit incredulous that I've survived this long after lung cancer.

I'm not sure exactly when these events occurred, but two of my most vivid memories relate to shopping. My friend Sandi and I always planned an annual trip to Minneapolis to celebrate our birthdays in February. We would have a nice dinner, see a play or go to a concert, and, of course, do some shopping. I remember, this year, wandering around Dayton's in downtown Minneapolis, always one of my favorite places to shop, looking at clothes. I thought a new outfit would give me a lift, but then I remembered the new blazer I'd found hanging in my mother's closet after she died, one that she had never had a chance to wear. Even though I was determined to fight, and to fight hard, some part of me just couldn't spend money on clothes, so I went home empty-handed. Another time I was shopping in Eau Claire. I needed a new spring jacket and wanted one with a zip-out lining. I found a great sale on exactly what I wanted and bought it, but then left it hanging in the closet for over a month with the tags still on it, so Wayne could return it—just in case . Finally, one day I cut off the tags and wore it, thinking, *I'm going to wear this jacket a long time.* It's still my favorite for cool Wisconsin fall days!

I've spoken little about my prayer life during this time, but it was intense. I felt an exceptionally close connection with God, one in which not only did I pray, but I felt the response, the strength that somehow, from somewhere, came to me. Some people believe there are angels all around us. Well, I believe that God sent a number of those angels to me in the disguise of the ordinary people around me. I hoped my family could feel the same, for daily I prayed for strength for them as well as for myself, strength to face whatever lay ahead for all of us. I offered not only prayers asking for strength, but prayers of thanksgiving, sometimes simply for helping me through the day, but also for bigger things, such as the day of my little "graduation" party in the oncology department. I had made it through chemotherapy. Now, that was something to be thankful for!

Looking at the calendar for this period, I see lots of babysitting days and many social events keeping us busy. Trips to the island, though, were especially important for the balance they provided. Sometimes there were interesting meetings that offered intellectual stimulation, but even more valuable were the opportunities for reflection and absorption of the beauty and peace of the island. During the winter I often sat looking out across the snow-covered meadow at the icy beauty of Lake Superior. Later, I watched the daffodils pop up, offering their bright, sunny promise of spring and warmer days. I played the piano and found a great deal of solace in making and listening to music. Playing the rhythmic, steady notes of a Beethoven sonata provided me with a sense of order and control that was missing in much of my life, while listening to the strains of a string quartet playing Dvorak could lift me up and help me soar away from my worries about cancer—and death.

Then there was, of course, the appointment with the surgeon, for finishing chemotherapy wasn't the end of treatment, just the end of step number two. There had been the diagnosis and the chemotherapy, but I still had surgery to go. Nevertheless, chemotherapy was finished, and I had survived with few difficulties.

There should have been a little respite between chemotherapy and surgery, but as I look at the calendar, I see bright yellow highlighted words repeated over a period of about two weeks. *Move*, it says. How can I have forgotten that? We'd agonized over it all winter. We had sold our house in Eau Claire several years earlier and had been living in an apartment downtown, right on the river. It was small, but I loved everything about it. But we

Gay J. Lindquist

had decided that the rent was too expensive, and we should find
something else. We had done a lot of looking and finally decided
on a townhouse that was just being constructed. Wayne had
watched it going up all winter and was excited about it, probably
because during construction he could see something positive
happening. I, on the other hand, didn't want to move and found
that was just one more thing to make my tears flow that spring.
I didn't want change. I wanted everything back like it had been.
But regardless of what I wanted, we had made a decision, and
the movers arrived with their truck on April 29, transporting
our possessions to a new place. The next day we went back to
clean the apartment, and when we finished I said, "Please, just
let me stay a while. I need to say 'good-bye' alone." As the door
closed behind Wayne, I sat down on the floor of the empty, clean
apartment and watched the sun stream across the balcony and in
through the windows for the last time. The shadows grew longer,
and once again the tears came. Too much was changing too fast!
I wanted to stop the clock!

As I turn the calendar over to May, I see *to Istanbul* written,
and then crossed out. The marvelous trip we had planned to
take, canceled. It says, *Gay—hospital 5:45 AM.* Instead of taking
a once-in-a-lifetime trip, I was going in for surgery to remove a
lobe of my lung, but tucked away in my closet was a surprise—a
tuxedo for Wayne's sixtieth birthday. It was meant to be more
than a gift. It said that we would still go places and do things. It
was a promise I was going to make—and keep!

Wayside# 2

Let's stop again by the river for a few moments of reflection. By this point on my journey, the ice had melted and the river was high and rushing rapidly on toward the sea. It was seemingly out of control, but carried with it, as I saw it, vitality and hope—hope for new life. Beds of sunny yellow daffodils, and even a few ruby red tulips, were starting to bloom along the bank. The trees lining the shore were filled with pale yellow buds, ready to burst into rich, green leaves. The world seemed alive with promise as I ended the medical treatment portion of my journey through cancer.

To anyone traveling this same road, I would say that it's important to seek knowledge, support, and comfort from whatever resources are available and most effective for you; these resources, however, may not be the same as what someone else thinks you need. You will probably be inundated with print materials from your oncology nurse and oncologist. They certainly can be helpful. Read them, but remember that you don't have to read them all at one time. That can be overwhelming! Read just what you're comfortable with. That's OK. View them as resource material, not an assignment that must be completed by a certain date. Look up things as you need information. Also, don't forget that reading something light with a little humor can go a long way toward making you feel better. I found that reading or hearing other people's stories was often helpful. I heard lots of horror stories about people who had died from lung cancer, but the one story I remember was about the uncle of a friend of ours who had had surgery for lung cancer twenty years earlier and was still going strong. That gave me the hope, whether realistic or not, that I needed at the time. I suppose that, at least in part, is why I am writing this—just to share my story, with its promise of hope, with others. Sometimes just knowing that someone had the same problem or the same fears helps to make you feel you're normal, and for most of us that is a comfortable feeling.

Thank people for their offers of help, but remember you don't have to accept them if you don't feel that you need or want them. Just thank people graciously and tell them you will let them know when they can help. On the other hand, don't hesitate to say yes if what they are offering is something that you need or want. People, I've found, rarely offer to help someone going through a difficult time if they don't mean it. Remember the times you have helped someone and how it has made you feel better. Other people like to experience that feeling as well. Someone, for whom you have never done anything special, may offer to help you, and you may wonder why. When that happens to me, I remember my mother once telling me that we don't always pay favors back to the same people that do them for us, but to someone else. It's OK. Accept the favors, and maybe you will be able to follow the concept in the movie, Pay it Forward. *Don't pay favors back, but pay them forward. Do good deeds for three more people. It sounds a little trite, but this could help to make the world a better place, and who doesn't want to do that?*

Hair. I suppose with all I said about my hair loss there must be some lesson to be learned there. Having talked with many people about this issue since my own hair loss, I've found that many people react as I did. One friend told me that she was never able to look in the mirror without her wig covering her bald head. Many people grieve and feel guilty that their grief is all out of proportion to the severity of the symptom. It is, I suppose, but on the other hand, for many of us, it is the one visible symptom that we have. Thus, the hair loss serves as a constant, visible reminder of our diagnosis. It's OK to grieve. Go ahead! Do it! Just try not to allow yourself to fixate on it. Decide what feels right for you and try it. If a wig is uncomfortable, try cute hats, baseball caps, scarves, a shaved head, or whatever feels right. If you would like a wig or a toupee but it seems too expensive, check with your oncology nurse or a local cancer center. There probably is a place in your community where you can borrow one. Maybe, like one of my friends, you will want hats and scarves for everyday but a wig for special occasions. Whatever you feel comfortable with is OK. This is about you, and you can make the decisions. There are enough things over which you have no control. Take charge wherever you can.

Sometimes your feelings may seem overwhelming. Express them. Talk to people, but remember that you don't have to talk to everyone about your problems and your feelings. Talk to whomever, whenever you want. Support groups are helpful for many people, but once again, go only if it seems it might be helpful. If you're not ready, or if you don't feel the need for it, don't go. You don't need to be a part of a group that will only make you feel worse. Writing is another wonderful way to express feelings. Keep a journal. Write letters. Write whatever is helpful to you.

I wish I could give more advice to those suffering from some of the uncomfortable side effects of chemotherapy, but because I experienced so few of them that it is difficult for me to do. I do know that figuring out the pattern, like I did with my leg pains, and then trying to find something I could do before it got bad was very helpful. Talk with your oncologist and oncology nurse about the problems you're experiencing and read about other people's experiences. Gather ideas, try them out, and then do what works best for you.

To caregivers and friends I would just say, "Be there." Let the person with cancer know that you care. It doesn't have to be much—just a phone call to say hi, a flower from the grocery store or your backyard, or a card saying, "I'm thinking of you." Sometimes it's hard to know what to say, but the most important thing is just to let someone know you're concerned. Offer to help, but don't be offended if you're turned down. Remember that for some people it's really important to be independent. Another simple thing to do is to tell someone if he or she looks good. Not if the person obviously doesn't, for anyone can see through that, but if he or she does, it could be a real boost to the ego. Even if someone looks extremely ill, there's usually something positive to say—maybe just that he's wearing a pretty shirt or she has a cute hat, but something. And one last thing—no one that I know wants to talk about the illness or treatment all the time. So many things in life are abnormal when you are living with cancer; it's wonderful to talk about "normal" things: grandchildren, politics, football, religion, or art—whatever you have always talked about with this person. After all, it's still the same person. I remember so many times thinking, Hey, this is still me! I'm not just a cancer patient! *It felt so good just to have a normal evening with friends. There were even times I could not think about having cancer!*

CHAPTER SIX

Surgery

May 1998

The dreaded morning arrived. I'd gone through chemotherapy with few problems and minimal pain and discomfort, but this would be different. The surgeon had forewarned me that chest surgery is very painful, saying, "I'm going to remove the entire lower right lobe of your lung so we get any remaining unseen cancer cells. That means a large incision, starting under your right breast and extending all the way around to your shoulder blade, and sawing through a rib." Now that sounded painful! I was going to have to experience all of that, yet I knew from my oncologist that the tumor was no longer evident on CAT scan or chest X-rays. I had to ask myself, *Why am I doing this if the tumor is already gone?* But the answer came quickly, as it had earlier when I'd decided on this treatment regime. *I want every possible chance to live to see those grandchildren grow up! I want the most aggressive treatment possible!*

Five AM. The alarm rang; we dressed quickly and were off to the hospital. It helped that I was admitted through the out-patient surgi-center, just as for other procedures, and that once again I saw familiar faces, but still I knew this time it was different. This was a major step. The admission process passed in a blur.

Then came the time when I had to remove my wig—something I hated to do, even then. "Here's a scrub cap," said a kind nurse as she held it out to me. It was like those I had worn many times as a nurse in the operating or delivery room and that made it easier. I was also concerned about being able to hear what people were saying to me, and was greatly relieved when a nurse said, "You can keep your hearing aids until just before you go into the operating room." The anesthesiologist visited. An IV was started, and suddenly I was trying to reassure Wayne, "I'll be fine," as they wheeled me away and into the pre-operative holding area. It had all gone so fast! I asked myself, *Am I ready?* But it didn't seem there was much choice in the matter at this point.

My surgeon was a very personable young man whom one of my friends had told me she had known when he was in second grade. That fact wasn't very comforting, but I had talked with one of my trusted colleagues at the School of Nursing where I had taught, and found that he had an excellent reputation as a chest surgeon. Nonetheless, when I met with him before the operation, I had asked him how many of these surgeries he had done, and if he felt my chances for long-term survival would be better if I went to Mayo Clinic two hours away in Rochester, Minnesota, instead of staying at Luther Midelfort, a Mayo satellite facility in Eau Claire. I remember feeling uncomfortable asking those questions, but I needed to ask in order to be a responsible patient. He assured me that he had done many of such surgeries with good results, and after some consideration, I had decided to have him do the surgery and to stay close to home. Still, when he stopped in to talk to me just before going into the operating room he asked, "Are you still sure you want me to do the surgery? It's not too late to cancel it and refer you to Rochester Mayo if you would feel more comfortable." By that time, of course, my decision had been made, and I assured him that I wanted him to do the surgery. "Let's do it, and get it over with!" I said. His just asking about it impressed me and only served to further increase my confidence in him. Also, a nurse that attended the church I used to belong to in Eau Claire stopped in to say that she was scheduled to be in my operating room. She asked, "Will you be uncomfortable having both me and a surgeon who belong to your old church in the operating room?"

"Not at all, "I replied quickly, "If anything, it is reassuring."

Then, suddenly, I was wheeled away—into the operating room. I looked around as they pushed me in, realizing I no longer had any control over what was happening. I remembered being wheeled in for a hysterectomy, and my days in the OR as a student nurse so many years ago. Somehow my nurse's mind was looking for the things that had changed and the things that still looked the same after all those years. In retrospect it seems a strange thing to be thinking about, but I suppose it was my way of escaping from the reality of what was about to happen to me. The anesthesiologist ended that escape, however, when he quietly explained what was going to happen and then said, "OK, Gay, now it's time for you to begin counting backwards from one hundred.

I remember saying, "One hundred, ninety-nine, ninety-eight …" and then heard someone calling my name, someone from someplace far, far away.

It was Tom, one of my former students, and I was in the recovery room. Now, here, I'm sure my memories are inaccurate, and my family may even laugh at my strange recollections of what happened, but once again, I remember that the bed was situated diagonally in the room. I found it difficult to realize it was all over. I may even have asked about that several times, just to be sure. It seemed that only a minute ago they had taken me into the operating room. I also remember that nothing hurt, and I felt amazed at that, even though I must have realized that it was only the medication that was keeping away the pain. I remember faces but little else of that immediate post-operative period. Wayne. Eric and Susie. My friend, Sandi. It was reassuring to see those much loved, but concerned, faces. They seemed to come and go, fade in and out, but I knew they were there. I remember Tom coming back and telling me that it was time for me to sit up on the edge of the bed. It seemed only minutes later, but I suppose it was several hours. I felt the chest tubes protruding from my chest wall, the IV tubing, and the monitor wires. *No way.* I thought, *I can't do it!* But then my old stubborn streak showed itself, and I remembered my mother saying that she thought my first words were, "I can do it myself!" *I can*, I thought. *I have to. I have to show everyone I can do it!* So, slowly, carefully, with helpful hands supporting me and adjusting my tubes, I sat on the edge of the bed. *I did it!* I thought. *My first step in recuperation! I'm going to make it. I'll show everyone!* But, I had to admit, lying down again, even on that unyielding hospital bed, was a wonderful and welcome relief.

Trying to recall that immediate post-operative period is a bit like looking back through a dense fog. I recall outlines and shapes, but it all is extremely hazy. One of my first concerns when I was fully awake was my hearing aids, and I felt a great sense of relief when I got them back quickly and could hear again. Probably not hearing well at first only added to the fogginess associated with the effects of the anesthesia. Everything seemed to lose its haze and look a little clearer when I could hear normally again, but I suppose that was mostly related to the anesthesia wearing off. One of my other early recollections was reaching up to touch my head and feeling relieved that the surgical scrub cap was still covering my bald head. I've never really thought of myself as particularly vain, but I must admit that I was a bit fanatical about my hair. I had packed my sleep cap, and one of my first requests, after my hearing aids, was for my sleep cap. Yikes, I guess I really was vain!

Memories of those next few days come tumbling back so fast I can scarcely write them down. The problem is that they come in no particular order. The first, and perhaps most significant, was the absence of pain during those first few days. I had had an epidural anesthesia that did a marvelous job of keeping the pain at bay. That, I'm sure, made it possible for me to begin getting up and moving around fairly quickly, even though I was still attached to chest tubes. I vividly recall feeling like I was on a tether. I was determined to recuperate quickly, and walked and walked in my room—but only as far as those chest tubes would allow.

The morning they removed the epidural catheter I was both pleased that I was making progress and apprehensive about how I would handle the pain. The nurses told me to be sure to ask for pain medication before it became severe, but I was torn between wanting to appear brave to everyone around me and longing for comfort. I quickly learned that my surgeon was right. This was painful surgery, combining the pain associated with intrusive surgery with that of an essentially broken rib. The nurses were also right that it really helps to "stay ahead of the pain," just as it had with my leg pains during chemotherapy. It was much easier for me to get up and move about when I asked for something before the pain became severe, and I certainly hoped that becoming active would speed my recovery.

I also remember the incentive spirometry. What an appropriate name! I would sit up as straight as I could, hold the spirometer in my hand, and seal my lips around the mouthpiece. Then I would inhale slowly and deeply, watch the piston go up the indicator column, hold my breath as long as I could, and slowly exhale. Each time I inhaled and watched that piston rise, I would try to make it go higher. I had a lot of incentive to do well, for once again I saw a test that I was going to pass, one at which I was going to excel. I suppose I have always been a bit competitive, but this was self competition, competing to do a better job than I had the last time, to do well so that I could go home and put this whole experience behind me.

I tried to be very patient with and supportive of the nursing students, but one of my negative memories is of the student who, several evenings after surgery, insisted that I put on my surgical support stockings when I went to bed. "But you still have chest tubes in!" she argued when I resisted. I understood she had been taught that support stockings are important to help prevent blood clots when a patient spends a great deal of time in bed following surgery, but I became irritated when she just couldn't grasp the fact that I had been up much of the day walking in my room. Later, a wonderfully mature night nurse, who could look beyond what it said in the textbook, removed my support stockings. How I appreciated that simple act.

I also remember another nurse checking the oxygenation level of my blood. She informed me the level was too low and that she would have to put me back on oxygen, even though I had not had any for several days. I knew, from the way I felt, that wasn't right and asked her, "Are you sure?" She checked it again said, "It's very low," so I agreed to have the oxygen turned on again, but I was more irritated than depressed that I was getting worse. I was sure there was absolutely nothing wrong with the oxygen level of my blood. I was lying there in my bed with a cannula stuck in my nose, watching some mindless TV series when she returned to my room, apologized profusely, and explained, "The batteries were too low." She checked it again. It was fine, and she removed the oxygen. In some strange way, I saw this as a small victory. Perhaps I was not only in competition with myself, but with the nurses as well. I needed to prove my competence and worth, not only to myself, but to the people around me.

Now I seem to have described myself as a difficult, ego-driven patient and I'm feeling a bit defensive. For the most part, at least in my memory, I was a *good* patient, being cooperative, doing what I was told, following the rules, and trying hard. I tried to be supportive of the nursing staff and, especially, the nursing students, always reassuring them that it was OK if they were a little slow or unsure of themselves. I only became *difficult* when someone didn't listen to me and could not, or would not, look at the whole situation and personalize whatever it said in the textbook or on the nursing care plan. Once again, control probably was an issue. Almost everything was beyond my control, except for pushing to get up, to walk, and do things that were uncomfortable. Consequently, there were a few situations where

I did assert myself—trying to regain at least a small degree of control.

It's only now, over a decade later, that I can look back on the situation and see that perhaps some of the students and young staff nurses were intimidated by having to care for me, a former nursing professor. I certainly didn't feel intimidating, only vulnerable and fearful of what the future might hold for me, but that may not be what they saw when they looked at me.

There is a funny memory, too. Hospital food is usually thought of as being tasteless, if not inedible, but the food at Luther was always excellent. I had enjoyed it many times in the hospital cafeteria and found it just as good when there as a patient. When looking over the menu after breakfast each morning, I would select whatever sounded good. There wasn't a lot of pleasure in my life just then, so I could see little sense in worrying about the caloric content of the food I ordered. My oncologist, as I mentioned earlier, was a small, very trim man who still makes me feel huge, even now, years later, when I go back for my annual checkups. One day, as I was finishing my chicken and mashed potatoes and gravy, with a piece of pie waiting for me that the whole world could see, he stopped in to say hi. He stood opposite me, chatting, chewing on a piece of raw cauliflower. I remember nothing of what he said to me, only that I was sure that was his lunch and he must think of me as a total pig. Oh, the strange things that our memories choose to hang on to!

One memory, especially, was full of hope. My car had well over a hundred thousand miles on it, and we were planning to replace it. I loved Hondas and had done some research on the Internet about styles and prices, and we had gone to a local dealer to look at them before I entered the hospital. I had decided what to buy, but we hadn't ordered it yet. Now, of course, Wayne would have been pleased to go to the dealer and order it for me while I was in the hospital, and, in retrospect, it probably would have provided a much-needed diversion for him, but no, I chose to do it myself. Therefore, one day, while sitting in my hospital bed, I called the dealer, asked for the salesperson I liked, and ordered the sportiest model Honda Accord coupe—complete with a V-6 engine, leather seats, and a spoiler! I don't know if all husbands would have been that obliging, but there were no complaints from Wayne. Partly it was that old *control* issue. I wanted to have control over something. Also, I'm sure it was because I am a woman. I wanted to show that gender has nothing to do with the ability to buy a car. Most importantly, though, I think it was a need for hope, hope for a future in which I was going to drive my sporty new car. Incidentally, it still looks great and drives like a dream—eleven years later!

The visits from family and friends did a great deal to raise my spirits. Wayne was there much of every day, always caring, saying just the right thing, offering just the right touch, and understanding my personal need for independence. He knew me well enough to let me be as independent as I could be. My dear son, Eric, would pop in at lunchtime with a big smile on his face, just to say hi, and often stop back for a more leisurely visit in the evening. My lovely daughter-in-law, Susie, also with a smile, visited often. They came in spite of their worries about Jackson. The whole family seemed optimistic, hopeful for the future. Perhaps they didn't feel as positive as they appeared, but it certainly helped not to have everyone projecting gloom and doom. Many friends, some close and others more distant, surprised me with their visits. One of the good things about all of these visits was that people showed concern for how I was feeling, but didn't just focus on that; they were able to go on to talk about their lives and ideas. That helped me to regain a much-needed sense of normalcy.

My two favorite times of the day were mail and flower deliveries. My room gradually filled with flowers—bouquets from local florists or the gift shop downstairs, and fragrant lilacs from friends' gardens. They all lifted my spirits, made me feel cared about, and gave me hope. A group of women friends gave me a huge planter filled with colorful annuals for the deck at our house on Madeline Island. Those flowers gave me joy and reminded me of that special group of friends for months to come. The cards, too, were overwhelming. I couldn't believe the number of cards I received—many from family and close friends, but also some from people that I really hadn't been in touch with for years. I loved all of them, but I also remember wondering if some of them thought that I wouldn't make it. Those thoughts only served to make me more determined to join the ranks of the survivors.

The most moving card of all didn't arrive during mail delivery. It was a Mother's Day card—not in the usual sense, but in the newspaper. Eric is a journalist and writes a viewpoint column called "Off Beat" every few weeks. Three days after surgery I saw his picture and name at the top of a column entitled "Killer Habit." It addressed the issue of teen smokers. I hope it was as moving to some of them as it was to me. Bear with me while I quote portions of it:

Let me drop all pretense of objectivity right away.

I think smoking stinks—literally and figuratively.

That long-held opinion was strengthened three days ago when my mom underwent surgery for lung cancer. It was the culmination of a four-month nightmare that included a series of unpleasant procedures to confirm the dreaded C-word diagnosis, nine weeks of chemotherapy, and related emotional turmoil for our whole family.

While we'll never be sure of the cause, smoking is the likely culprit even though she hasn't touched a cigarette in more than ten years, never smoked more than a pack a day, and quit smoking several other times—once for seven years.

He went on, very powerfully, at least to this biased mother's ears, to speak to teenagers about the consequences of smoking and to urge them to quit. Now! He ended by saying:

> *My mom may have lost a lobe of her lung, but she's lucky—her cancer was caught early, so her prognosis looks good.*
>
> *Our family is lucky because we didn't lose her—a grim prospect we couldn't avoid pondering this spring, especially after seeing one of my mom's best friends die of lung cancer just three and a half years ago.*
>
> *Now we desperately hope Monday's surgery removed the last trace of cancer from my mom's body forever and that she achieves her next goal—going home from the hospital by Mother's Day. There could be no sweeter gift than going home cancer-free.*
>
> *So even though it's a few days early, let me take this opportunity to say, "Happy Mother's Day, Mom. May you enjoy many more."*

Perhaps the only gift sweeter than going home cancer-free is having a son like that. What better Mother's Day card and gift could any mother ever receive?

CHAPTER SEVEN

Culprit

May 1998

That night, after reading Eric's column, I lay on my firm, unyielding hospital bed futilely trying to find a comfortable position for sleep, thinking about what he had said. Cigarettes—the culprit, he'd called them. *Why in the world had I ever started smoking them?!?*

I remembered my mom, a very conservative Christian, a teetotaler. One of her brothers died from lung cancer, another from complications of emphysema. Both had smoked. She hated smoking, and I did all I could for years to hide my nasty habit from her. When we visited them I would volunteer to run an errand just so I could sneak a cigarette. Even in my own home, when they visited us, I would go outside in the cold or sneak a smoke in our bedroom—carefully blowing smoke out an open window. Did I really think she didn't know I smoked? That she couldn't smell it on my breath, on my clothes, on my hair? Surely not! She believed cigarette smoking was not only a dirty, unhealthy habit, but it was *bad,* and what "kid" doesn't want to hide from her parents the fact that she is being naughty? I felt guilty then, just remembering.

And speaking of feeling guilty! Not only had I smoked, but I had smoked while I was pregnant and an obstetrics nurse! We didn't have all the warnings in 1960 that we have now, so I wasn't aware of how significantly smoking during pregnancy could increase the chances for a low birth-weight baby or pre-term delivery. I must, though, have had some idea it wasn't a good thing to be doing, for I can still remember the tiny gold cigarette case I carried in the pocket of my pure white nurse's uniform. It was flat, barely showing in my pocket. It had the engraving of a flower on the top that I often traced with my finger. It held just five cigarettes—my personal allotment for the day. Our son *was* born three weeks early and only weighed five pounds and seven and one-half ounces, but he has grown into a tall, smart, athletic man. When he was in high school he used to say that if I hadn't smoked maybe he would have been a pro basketball player. I know he was kidding, but I couldn't help but ask myself, *Does he really think that in some way I limited his potential?* I certainly hope not. I cringed when I remembered him telling me how he always hated the smell of smoke and how, as a child, he even hid cigarettes from me.

I chastised myself further, remembering that I hadn't been a kid when I started smoking. I was married, a nurse. My new husband was studying for a year in seminary. It was a strange time to pick up such a deadly habit, but I did. There were such fun times associated with smoking—all of us smoking, drinking, and laughing at parties during graduate school and our first years in Eau Claire. Almost everyone smoked. It had seemed the *normal* thing to do—except when we were with my parents.

I remember when the health warnings started to come out. Wayne and I both tried to quit—time after time after time! He could always quit so easily, but it was agony for me. I could remember wanting a cigarette so badly I could hardly stand it. It was especially agonizing to go without one with a drink or after a meal. I would quit for a week and suddenly, one night at midnight, drive to the store to buy a pack. We would both quit, and then stop on the way to a party to pick up a pack. We'd just smoke at the party and then quit again, we would promise ourselves. Wayne could do that, and I resented it. How could it be so easy for him and so impossible for me? It wasn't fair! Later, after I was teaching in the School of Nursing, I would quit for the whole summer and then find myself madly digging for change during registration week and rushing across campus to the student center to buy a pack from a vending machine. I would quit and not want to admit to anyone that I had started again, so I would stand outside in the rain or freezing cold—trying to hide my filthy habit, and my failure. Yes, I mused, more than wanting to hide the habit, I had not wanted to admit to my friends and colleagues that I had failed—again.

I reassured myself that I had tried everything. Cold turkey had never worked very well, although I tried it many times. It always found me back in my car, headed out to buy a pack at some odd hour of the day or night. Then, to save the inconvenience of those trips, I started hiding cigarettes. I'd keep a pack hidden in the back of a drawer or in the glove compartment of my car. *I won't open the pack,* I would promise myself; *It's just there in case of emergency.* Well, I must have had a lot of emergencies, for that didn't work either. Never did many days pass without me opening that pack, and then it would be empty—and soon replaced. I tried carrot sticks. When I craved a cigarette, I would just eat a carrot stick instead. Somehow a carrot stick with my coffee after dinner didn't work either! Then there were the straws, carefully cut off to just the length of a cigarette. I would just hold the straw between my index and middle finger and inhale slowly, luxuriously. Exhale—imagining the wispy trail of smoke drifting off into the distance. Ahhh!!!!!! Well—it may have been better than a carrot, but satisfy the craving for a cigarette? No way! Once during that phase, I recalled the down-to-earth, elderly Scottish mother of a friend of ours saying, "Aggh! What on God's good earth do you think you are doing?" as I inhaled on my straw.

I sheepishly replied, "I'm trying to quit smoking."

"Well, girl, if you want to quit, just quit!" she declared. Oh, if only it had been that simple!

Then I would just give up and not try for a while, simply admit to myself, *I'm a smoker and I can't quit!* I would once again just enjoy a cigarette, and *almost* not feel guilty. After all, it wasn't really my fault. I was addicted before I knew how bad it was for your health. When we were building our house on Madeline Island, it was such a good excuse for a break—sitting on the roof, tar staining my jeans and smeared on my face for good measure, having a smoke—literally feeling on top of the world. Pacing outside the hospital, while taking a break from my bedside vigil with a critically ill parent. Sitting on the deck of our unfinished house, looking out at Lake Superior and sipping an icy martini. Good times. Stressful times. Ordinary times. All of them—I had a cigarette!

But I also remembered how much I had wanted to quit. I remembered the deaths of my uncles. I read articles about the dangers of smoking. So I would try another program. Some stop-smoking aids became available to help you quit, but you had to have a prescription, and I didn't even want to admit to my physician that I smoked. I, a nurse, actually lied on my health history. Once again that old *I can do it myself* attitude would surface, and I would try again.

Finally, a friend on Madeline Island gave me a little book. I don't remember the name of it, or what organization published it, but it outlined a quit smoking program. I do remember that there was a little demon in the book and his name was Pat. You had to read a portion of the book every day, and Pat would try to convince you to smoke. He really was a little demon, and I could identify with him so well. But I wasn't going to let him get the best of me. The program worked! Gradually I decreased the tar and nicotine in my cigarettes, decreased the number of cigarettes a day, and then gradually smoked less of each cigarette. Finally, only taking a few puffs, I was to put my cigarette butts in a peanut butter jar. I did as instructed when I reached the day of *NO MORE! I'M FINISHED* and poured water in the jar. Then, each time I had a mad craving for a cigarette, I would pull out my jar, screw off the top and inhale deeply. *Phew*!! That, finally, was enough to make even me not want another cigarette. Actually, it was strange, but that time it was easy. I never went back, never had another cigarette. Now that's not to say that I never thought about it. Once in a while, out of the blue, I would think about how nice it would be to have a cigarette, but I never did. I quit. But, of course, it was too late. The foundation had already been laid for the monster that had grown inside of me. These thoughts not only popped into my mind as I lay in bed that night after reading Eric's column, but they had been there as I sat watching the poison drip into my arm during chemotherapy, and continued as I struggled with pain following surgery. They came unbidden and made me feel guilty. *I brought it on myself,* I would think. *I was too smart to have let this happen to me!* But I had. *Oh, if only I could have met Pat years earlier,* I thought as I finally drifted off into a restless sleep.

CHAPTER EIGHT

Celebrations

May 1998

Oh, how I hoped to be home for Mother's Day! It was six days after surgery, and the surgeon had assured me that most patients can go home that soon. I felt pretty good—as long as I took pain medications on time and got plenty of rest, for I did find that I tired easily. There was one problem, however. My chest tubes wouldn't stop draining! They couldn't discharge me as long as I had chest tubes in, so Mother's Day, my first one with *two* grandchildren, was spent in my hospital room, We celebrated it along with Wayne's birthday that fell on the same day. I was amazed to see just how festive my family could make it seem. We, of course, already had the flowers, and cards covered the walls, but they added the touch of nonalcoholic champagne and a family-favorite chocolate cake complete with multicolored candles carefully placed by Katie at my bedside. We feasted on a bucket of Kentucky Fried Chicken and plenty of side dishes, and somehow it seemed that I had never tasted a better holiday meal. There were presents, even including a surprise for Wayne from me that I had carefully packed before I left home—just in case I didn't make it home in time for his birthday. He was surprised when I had a package for him, and looked puzzled as he opened my gift for him: a cummerbund and bow tie to go with his new birthday tux. There it was again, that promise of a future together—doing things, going places! It was a wonderful day, in spite of my disappointment at not getting to go home, one filled with gifts and laughter, but most importantly, love. There are pictures of that day in a family photo album—one of me with wig, earrings, makeup, and a broad smile!

Mother's Day in the hospital

There are pictures of all of us smiling, even baby Jack. We probably all had our personal fears about the future, but I don't think we worried it might be one of our last family holidays together. It was another turning point, a time to look forward. We were over a big hurdle. However, there was still my recuperation, then Jack's surgery to go. Nevertheless, we were going to make it—as an intact family!

But then I was impatient. I was ready to *go home*! I've always liked to drink water and I am probably the only person I know that ever went on the water diet and didn't have to increase their water intake. So what had I been doing while sitting around a hospital room all day every day with someone always keeping my pitcher full of cold, fresh water? I'd been drinking it. Like crazy! One morning my surgeon stopped in and I moaned a bit, I'm afraid, about the fact that my chest tubes wouldn't stop draining. "Isn't there something you can do?" I asked in frustration.

He looked at my chart, mused for a moment, and then said, "I've never told a patient to drink less water, but perhaps you should cut back on your intake a bit. That might help." Now, you might think that somehow, with my nursing background, that might have entered my mind at some point, but it hadn't. So I started drinking less water, and lo and behold, the amount of drainage from my chest tubes steadily decreased until it almost stopped. Finally, the surgeon said those wonderful words I had been waiting to hear, "Let's take them out." Music to my ears! Certainly the small amount of discomfort involved was well worth it. That was mid-morning. I was told that I would have to wait several hours, but then, if all was well, I could go home.

At last I could get out of that room. Except for calling Wayne to tell him to come and get me, eating lunch, and resting a bit, I walked back and forth, up and down the halls, until I was discharged. I enjoyed chatting with people and seeing something different, but most of all I experienced a marvelous sense of freedom. I was rid of my tether! The agreed-upon number of hours passed, and one of my former students came in to tell me that I could go. Even though it still hurt to stretch and bend, I dressed quickly, gathered all my stuff together, put on my call light, and announced into the intercom, "I'm ready to go!" A nurse came in with a wheelchair, but I said I didn't want to use it.

The old days, when legally you had to discharge patients in wheelchairs, were over, but she asked, "Are you sure? It's a long way down to the front door." I was sure. I felt a little tired, but strong. She walked beside me as I walked down that hall for the last time. All the staff came out to say good-bye and wish me well, and there were even a few hugs. Suddenly, there was Wayne in the car he had pulled around to the front door. What a happy sight! I took a deep breath of the fresh, sweet spring air, said good-bye to the nurse, and we drove home—on to the next phase of this tortuous journey.

CHAPTER NINE

Recuperation

May–July 1998

As I look back at those old calendars again, I see that only two days after I was discharged we went up to our house on Madeline Island, one hundred eighty miles from Eau Claire. I'm sure I must have longed just to be in our house, to gaze at the lake, to offer thanksgiving in the place where God has always seemed closest to me. I needed, as well, to ask for strength and courage for whatever lay ahead. I felt cautiously optimistic regarding the future, but that dark cloud of doubt about my long-term survival certainly hadn't disappeared. It was hard to forget the grim statistics, and I yearned for the island. It was where I had gone after the funeral of my dear friend, Jan, and after the deaths of my parents. Madeline Island was where I needed to be. Also, I wanted to go to our church—partly to worship, but also to see people and show them I was doing OK.

It was unseasonably warm when we arrived on the island, and most of the daffodils in our meadow had faded, but a few of them still showed their cheery little yellow faces. The hummingbirds were back, flitting back and forth, eagerly awaiting their sugary nectar. The chives, mint, and lavender were coming up, adding fragrance to the warm spring air. Bright yellow marsh marigolds bloomed merrily in the creek, patches of deep purple violets carpeted the woods, and clusters of tiny blue forget-me-nots brightened the roadsides. Only the brown of the withered daffodils reminded me of death and the circle of life. Otherwise the world seemed full of hope and the promise of spring—exactly what I needed at that point in my journey.

Things were going well with my recuperation, but it certainly wasn't all easy. Pain was probably the most difficult thing to manage. The pain pills helped pretty well in the daytime, but sleeping was difficult. I had always slept on my side, and it was extremely difficult to find a comfortable position for sleep. I can remember going to the guest room several nights because I was afraid my restlessness would disturb Wayne. Then I would toss and turn in the unfamiliar bed, looking out at the cedar trees and starry skies outside the window, thinking how unattractive and unappealing I must seem to Wayne—a bald head, a huge scar on my side, and not even able to find a comfortable position to lie in bed beside him.

There was also the problem of bras. They hurt—a lot! I was reminded of that by looking at the only picture of me with my nearly bald head, one I had asked Wayne to take, realizing that someday I might want some kind of visual record of my hair loss. I was wearing a bathing suit. Most of the picture has been cut away, for I have never looked my best in a bathing suit, but I remember why I was wearing it. It didn't hurt!

Gay with bald head and bathing suit

There was nothing cutting into my tender side. It was at that time I discovered soft cotton, fasten-in-the-front sports bras, the only kind I could tolerate wearing for quite a while.

Even though the old calendar shows that we quickly resumed a fairly busy social schedule, I remember that I tired easily. I became impatient with that, especially when it was spring and I wanted to get plants out and have everything looking nice by Memorial Day. I couldn't lift heavy pots and bags of soil, but I could give Wayne directions and place the plants in the soil and feel the moist, nourishing soil between my fingers. Not only did I want the joy of seeing the plants in place, but there was also something about those small plants that showed such promise for the future.

But we couldn't stay on the island. We had to return to Eau Claire, for I had appointments for chest X-rays and a post-operative visit with the surgeon. I don't recall any particular anxiety associated with that visit, for I thought I was doing OK surgically. My biggest concern was pain control and being able to sleep comfortably. He changed my pain pills, removed some stitches and assured me, "You're doing fine." Then there was the first post-op visit to my oncologist, preceded by a now-familiar CAT scan. Again I was reassured that everything looked good. A schedule was set up for my follow-up visits, and I was on my way.

We saw a few friends, shopped to stock up on supplies for a summer on the island and, strangely enough, I had a manicure. Now, manicures were one thing that I never had spent money or time on, but I visited my long-term hairdresser and had her give me a manicure. I didn't have any hair for her to cut or style, but she still could help me to feel a little more beautiful. When she finished, she styled my wig a bit, gave me a big hug, and I was happily ready to take off again for the island, feeling just a little more attractive and more ready to face the world.

Eric and his family always come to the island for Memorial Day weekend, and that year was no exception. It was Jack's first visit to the island. We seem to have taken an inordinate number of pictures that year, of every combination of us. There is at least one of everyone holding Jack—on the beach, in the house, on the deck—everywhere. There are posed pictures of family groups and candid shots of Katie at play—one playing with the wig from the dress-up box. One of my favorite pictures of all time comes from that weekend; it's taken from the edge of the high bank that stretches across the front of our property, looking down on the beach at Eric and Katie writing their names with sticks in the sand. They made marks that have long since washed away, but those warm memories will last forever.

Katie and Eric on Madeline Island Beach

There was a cloud over the weekend, though. Jack was scheduled for a cardiac catheterization in a few weeks, and he would probably have surgery shortly after that. We had all been reassured that he would be fine, but he was only three months old, still so tiny, and this would be a very involved surgery. We all probably had thoughts about the possibility of something going wrong. *What if his tiny body couldn't survive the surgery? How many more trips would he have to this island that we all loved?* But those thoughts were much too painful for any of us to articulate.

Grandpa Wayne and Jackson

Besides, the flowers were blooming on the deck, and buttercups added their note of sunshine to the scene as we watched a newborn fawn follow his mother across the meadow on his spindly little legs. All of this served to offer us hope.

Looking back at the pictures of me that weekend, I see that I'm smiling and happy, but on closer look, I see that my eyes are tired and I undoubtedly still enjoyed a nap when the kids took one. My pain, however, was beginning to diminish. Actually, it's hard to remember how and when that occurred. It was just a gradual thing that spring and early summer. It grew fainter. I took pain pills less frequently, and then at some point I realized the pain was gone. My scar wasn't, though, and I remember shopping for a new swimsuit that summer—one with a higher back that would cover more of my scar. I had an old abdominal scar but that was not right out there for the world to see. This one I needed to hide! I wasn't ready to discuss its cause with the world. Over the years, however, it has gradually become less and less apparent, until now it's barely visible.

A few weeks later we returned to Eau Claire. It was a big week! Jack's baptism was Sunday, and once again we have many pictures to record the day—family groups with Jack in his beautiful baptismal gown and Katie in her pretty flowered dress, Susie's family, and Eric and Susie's friends with their children.

Grandma and Grandpa Barber; Susie, Jackson, and Eric; Grandma and Grandpa Lindquist; and Katie

All of these pictures make me smile, but especially one of me where I am standing in a new dress bought especially for the occasion, evidently feeling that I would be around long enough to wear it, and standing by my shiny new car. I have a broad smile on my face and for the first time my eyes don't really look weary.

Gay and her new Honda

The fatigue returned, though, for when we babysat for Katie and Jack, I got tired, and not only wanted, but needed, a nap as much as they did. This, though, was a happy kind of tired. How I loved caring for those two precious little children! Katie stayed overnight when Eric and Susie took Jack up to the Twin Cities for his cardiac catheterization. The same day I had an X-ray and saw my surgeon again. He told me all was fine and discharged me from his care. Jack, on the other hand, was scheduled with a different surgeon, a cardiac surgeon, who would repair the five defects in his heart. What a bittersweet day!

Then it was back to the island where we had dinners with friends and overnight guests. There was a church council meeting, the preparation of committee and council reports for the annual meeting, and it was my month for Altar Guild and preparation for communion. Certainly, parts of life were beginning to regain a sense of normalcy.

One Sunday at church I slipped into the pew beside a friend who also was battling cancer. She had just completed a second round of chemotherapy and had lost all of her hair. She was one of those brave ones I mentioned earlier who never wore a wig. She had chosen to show her bald beauty to the world. I admired her for that. Now her hair was coming back, and was probably about an inch long all over her head. She leaned over and whispered in my ear, "I'll bet your hair is just as long as mine. Why don't you take that wig off?"

I frowned at her and said, "I'm not sure I'm ready for that, but … I'll think about it." That afternoon I thought about Mary and how pretty she had looked. I took my wig off and looked in the mirror. I ran my fingers through my short hair and tried to fluff it up a bit. She was right; mine was about the same length as hers. Could I leave it off now? I felt the back. It was curly! My hair has always been straight as a stick. I looked carefully at the color. It was dark brown, like it used to be, not faded from years of being out in the sun. *There's not even as much gray as there was*, I thought, *and besides, short, spiky hair is in style this summer. Maybe I should leave it off.* I stood there, looking for a minute, and then put the wig back on a stand in the back of my closet shelf—the place where it stands to this day. I'm not sure why it's still there—superstition, perhaps. If I give it away, will I need it again? I don't know, but I think I'll leave it there—just in case (even though it wouldn't have enough gray in it to match anymore!).

Soon it was the Fourth of July, which is a big event on Madeline Island. Katie, dressed in a brand new navy blue dress with sailor collar and a bright red scarf around her neck, rode in a little red wagon in the "wagon train." Susie pushed Jack in his brightly decorated stroller, and I walked along beside. There was something special about walking the whole parade route that year.

I was showing the world I could do it. I was a cancer survivor! I fondly recalled that walk several years later the first time I walked laps in the American Cancer Society's Relay for Life.

Fourth of July Parade on Madeline Island

Katie and Grandma after the parade

During that Fourth of July weekend our family smiled, laughed, went to the beach where Katie giggled and splashed delightedly in the water, had a picnic, and did all the things you should do on Independence Day, but in the back of our minds was another dark cloud—apprehension about Jack. Now it wasn't an abstract fear; it was real. Surgery was scheduled in a week. We all thought of that as we snapped his picture in his grandfather's strong hands with the bright blue sky as a background. As the shutter on my camera snapped, I silently prayed the same prayer I had offered often that spring, *Gracious and loving God, keep Jackson safe. Bring him health. If you must take one of us, dear God, take me! I thank you for the life I've had. Please let his be as long and full as mine. Amen.* That picture stands on a shelf in our island bedroom to this day—signifying both the fear and the hope of that time.

Jackson on Madeline Island

Soon it was time for Katie to come stay with us again, for her parents were off to Minneapolis with Jack. She knew what was happening and understood that he was going to have holes and valves fixed in his heart, but she had difficulty comprehending it all. "What if he … *dies?*" she asked me, her voice small and hesitant.

I felt my heart seize, and wanted to cry, but I assured her, "The doctors are very good. They will fix his heart, and he'll be just fine!" *Please, God, guide their hands. Keep him safe!* I prayed silently as I gave her a big hug. I had a book about a little girl whose baby sister goes to the hospital for surgery. We read it over and over. In fact, it was a favorite of hers for years, and later became a favorite of Jack's.

It seemed that it was forever from the time we knew Jack had gone to the operating room until the phone rang. It was Eric. "It's over. He's in the recovery room and doing fine," he said. We all, including Katie, let out a big sigh of relief and had a family hug. *Thank you, God!* I prayed silently. But then, an hour or so later, the phone rang again. This time Eric's voice had a different sound—tense, worried. "There's too much bleeding," he said. "They've taken him back to the operating room." I felt the world collapsing all around me. *He can't die*, I thought. *It's supposed to be me, not him! I've had sixty good years. He hasn't even had one.* I didn't want to die. I had fought my battle against cancer hard, but this wasn't fair. If it had to be one of us, it had to be me! Wayne must have seen that I was going to have difficulty coping with this and trying to support Katie, for he just quietly said, "Why don't we go to the playground for a while, Katie?"

I went out to the balcony of our townhouse and looked out across the hills, feeling empty, stunned. I couldn't even pray. I just stood there. Then, suddenly, I knew what I had to do. I picked up the phone and called my dear friend and pastor, Marina. I don't even know if I was coherent, just that I spilled out my aching heart to her and asked for her prayers. Just the knowledge that she was praying too seemed to draw a blanket of calm around me. After hanging up the phone I just sat there, breathing in the smell of freshly mown grass, feeling a sense of peace and hope.

It wasn't too long before the phone rang again, and it was Eric, who sounded much relieved. Jack was back in the recovery room. They had found the problem, fixed it, and everything looked fine. Once again, we took Katie to see her little brother attached to wires and tubes in the ICU, a scene becoming all too familiar to our family. The surgeon stopped for a post-operative visit while we were there. I don't remember his words, only his hands. They looked enormous, and I marveled at the fact that those huge hands had repaired Jackson's tiny heart. From that point on, his recovery went fairly smoothly, and it was time for him to join me in the recuperation phase. I thanked God for saving Jack—and also for not taking me. I wasn't ready. I had a lot of living left to do!

Wayside # 3

When I reached this portion of my journey, we no longer lived on the river, so my spot of reflection moved—north to Madeline Island. I often sat in my white Adirondack chair overlooking Chebomnican Bay in Lake Superior. The daffodils in our meadow had faded away and been replaced by the deep purple lupine and the cheery white daisies of summer. The world was lush and full of beauty, but I knew that beauty was fleeting. The lupine, like the daffodils, would fade and die. Some would bloom again in the spring, but others would not survive. I thought about having cancer, and wondered if I would be one of the survivors. What season of life is this for me? *I asked silently.* Surely, I thought, I can't be in the autumn of my years! I have too many things I want to do, too much to look forward to. *But before looking ahead, I needed to reflect, to see what lessons could be learned from the surgery and recuperation phase of my journey.*

What from these reflections might be helpful to others dealing with similar experiences? First of all, if you are dealing with cancer, ask questions when you're unsure about some aspect of treatment. It's OK. Don't worry that your question might sound stupid. You need to understand what is happening and why. If you don't understand, ask again.

Try hard—even when it hurts. Push yourself a bit. The more you move, the more you do your deep breathing exercises, the faster you will feel better. You don't have to be a martyr about it, however. Make sure that you manage your pain so that you can do the things you need to do to get better. Don't feel like a failure when you ask for pain medication in the hospital, or when you take it after you go home. That pain medication can be your ticket to a faster recuperation.

Get involved in life again, as quickly as you can. Don't just focus on yourself. Hopefully, others won't have to deal with additional serious issues like I did with Jackson's birth and heart defect, but I do think that, in some strange way, that was all helpful. How could I focus only on myself when this new precious baby was dealing with such serious problems?

Don't forget rest. Balance it with activity. It takes your body time to repair and rebuild after any kind of major surgery. Don't feel guilty! Take that nap when you need it. You may feel tired for longer than you expect. That's not unusual, so try not to get discouraged. Do some of those things you've always wanted to do but have never taken time for. Read those books in your "to read" pile, catch up on photo albums, even give yourself permission to watch a favorite old movie in the afternoon. It's OK. You deserve it!

Probably most importantly, try to use this portion of your journey through life as a real learning experience. Accept the fact that you are mortal, and make the most of each day. None of us know if we have hours or years to live, whether we have cancer or not. It sounds a little hackneyed, but take time to smell the herbs growing in your garden; taste the tang of the first crisp apple of fall; feel the silky softness of a newborn's skin; look at spring's first daffodil, appreciating each individual petal; and listen, really listen, to your favorite violin concerto, jazz, or country ballad. My flowers and music, whether listening to it or playing the piano, brought great comfort to me and offered me a wonderful way to express my feelings.

Families and friends, I think, can learn the same lessons. You also need to understand what the treatment options are and what to expect. Don't be afraid to ask questions. Encourage your friend or relative to keep trying to deep breathe, walk, or whatever it takes to recuperate—even when it is hard. Sometimes a little encouragement and support can make the journey a lot easier. It's also important for you not to be consumed by what is happening. Stay involved in life, and take care of yourself. I will always vividly remember a former student sending me home from the ICU one night when my mother was extremely ill. She reminded me of one of the lessons that I had taught her: You must take care of the caretaker. She instructed me to go home and to do something that I enjoyed—watch a favorite old movie, have a drink—anything that would give me a break.

One of the most difficult lessons to grasp is that this encounter with cancer can provide an opportunity to enrich your life and not just be a painful experience. You, too, don't know how much time you have with your loved one—or on this earth, for that matter. Think about your priorities and spend quality time with your loved ones, whether you have days, weeks, or years together.

CHAPTER TEN

Beyond

July 1998–Present

Gradually, life resumed the usual patterns. My energy increased, as did my lung capacity. I found it amazing how quickly the human body adapts to the loss of a lobe of lung. A few weeks after surgery I seemed to have almost no problem with shortness of breath, even when climbing the long flight of stairs up our bank from the beach. My hair grew out—slowly. Katie had a fourth birthday party on the island—complete with a pink frosted Barbie Doll cake and a ride from friends in their red Volkswagen bug convertible.

Katie on her fourth birthday

Then Wayne and I went on a trip. We traveled through Iowa on a nostalgic journey, visiting the farm where I had grown up, the small surrounding rural towns, the church where we were married, and the graves where my parents and other relatives are buried. We visited some of my cousins and returned to the Rocky Mountains we love. We drove through the shimmering golden aspens, something we had often talked about, but had never done. Now, I think, we realized that we might not have forever. We needed to do some of the things now that we had always wanted to do.

During the previous few months I had been so consumed with thinking about my diagnosis and treatment and Jack's heart problems that I hadn't really thought about the economic issues involved until the bills started coming in. They were astronomical! I would look at bills that itemized tests, equipment, supplies, and physician fees, and, even though I had been involved in the health care industry my entire adult life, I was amazed. Then, more than ever, I realized why I had put so much time and energy into taking nursing students abroad and teaching students on campus about other health care delivery systems, systems that provided universal health care to their citizens. I sat at my desk, looking out at Lake Superior, and smiled as I remembered my students talking about their home visits with British Health Visitors to new mothers. "*Everyone* gets prenatal care and well-baby visits, too!" they exclaimed in amazement. As they studied health care statistics it had become increasingly apparent to them how important it is for everyone to have access to good health care. I thought about the statistics that show huge numbers of people in our own country without health insurance. How could those uninsured ever cope with an illness like this without eventually having to declare bankruptcy? It made me feel incredibly thankful that we had good health insurance.

The colored leaves of fall fell, and snow covered the ground. I felt good. Optimistic—*most* of the time. Christmas came, and

Katie and I made our first gingerbread house, a tradition we carried on for years. Jack grew stronger, looking like a healthy little boy, not a baby, dressed in his dark pants and vest, white shirt, and tie in our Christmas pictures that year. My six months X-ray and checkup with the oncologist showed a good report. We had much to be thankful for that Christmas.

There were moments, though. I'd get a headache that wasn't relieved quickly by aspirin. *Is it a brain tumor?* Pains in my joints. *Is it in my bones?* I've had headaches all my life and I knew that bone cancer is more likely to show itself through an unusual fracture or pain in long bones, not joints, but still—my logical nurse's mind didn't always seem to function very well. Most of the time I felt positive and lucky, but I couldn't quite get over being super sensitive to every little ache and pain. These were things I could never share with anyone, even Wayne, until they were magically gone and I felt fine again. Those moments have gotten further and further apart over the years, but once in a while, out of the blue, there they are again.

Gradually, I began to feel that perhaps it was safe to plan for the future, maybe even a long one. But I wasn't sure. How could I be? Those grim statistics still popped, unbidden, into my head. I came to realize that you can't put everything off until tomorrow when you don't know, as none of us ever do, how many tomorrows you will have. So we scheduled that cruise we had planned, which would have left on the morning of my surgery. On April 19, 1999, eleven months after my surgery, we flew from Minneapolis to Athens, Greece. We went to Greece, Israel, and Turkey, finally going to Istanbul, where we were to have gone the May before. It was even more wonderful than we had anticipated; perhaps we appreciated it all even more than we would have the year before. Wayne looked handsome in that tuxedo I had given him for his sixtieth birthday. He did wear it, we did go places together—and we still do!

Wayne and Gay at Ephesus, Turkey

But even on that wonderful cruise, there were moments. I developed bronchitis that became so severe I had to go to the ship's doctor. I vividly remember answering the questions on the health history. Lung cancer. One year ago. I saw *the look* again—on the faces of the nurse and physician. I'm sure they hoped I wasn't having some major recurrence now, on their watch. During happy hour, while friends gathered for drinks, I went down to the ship's infirmary and had a respiratory treatment. I'd never had anything like that before in my life. *Is this normal?* I would ask myself. *Are the guarded looks on their faces justified?* I didn't know. But my symptoms disappeared almost as suddenly as they came, and I was quite sure that all was OK. Then, at Ephesus, while looking at the incredible sights, I sprained my ankle. I don't think that even I could twist my post-cancer brain into thinking that a sprained ankle was somehow cancer related, but I may have tried. Overall, that trip was one of those once-in-a-lifetime experiences. It was fantastic, but I did become aware of an increased vulnerability. I was still me, but not quite the same person I once had been.

Now, our grandchildren are growing up. We no longer have an apartment in Eau Claire, but have purchased a small house in Naples, Florida, to enjoy during the winters. I'm singing in a large church choir down here, and we're enjoying the cultural opportunities this wonderful city has to offer. There has been no evidence of recurrence or metastasis at any of my checkups. My visits to the oncologist have gradually decreased from bi-weekly to, finally, once a year. Each one of those changes felt like a graduation, and I gave thanks to God.

So, my journey has continued. It has not always been smooth, however. Eight years ago on a routine visit to my oncologist, when I anticipated our usual cheery chat, he told me that my chest X-ray looked great, but frowned as he looked at my lab results. "What's the problem?" I asked hesitantly.

"Well ..." he said, "your white blood count doesn't look quite right. I'd like to do another blood test." So I had more blood drawn and then waited until I could talk to him the next day. "You have a very mild form of CLL," he stated.

"CLL?" I repeated numbly.

"Chronic Lymphocytic Leukemia," he replied. Leukemia! That was the only word I could hear. He went on to explain it is very common, and that many people have it and it's not even diagnosed. "I have many patients who have had it for years and have no problems. You have no symptoms, and it requires no treatment," he assured me. "It may never require any kind of treatment." I readily accepted his reassuring words of "no symptoms, no treatment," but wondered how I was going to tell my family about this. I left the clinic, got into my car and turned, not toward Eric and Susie's house, but once again toward Carson Park and the lake—just to sit, stare at the tranquil water, think, and pray. Somehow, while the children played after dinner that night, I found the words to tell Wayne, Eric, and Susie that I had CLL, and to try to reassure them with the words I had heard from my oncologist. After we returned to the island, however, I quickly went to the internet to seek out information about CLL. Much to my relief, all of the sources agreed, "If mild, with no symptoms, no treatment is required." So far all has gone as expected. It has not progressed. I have had no symptoms and, thus, have required no treatment. It's just one more thing I've added to my list of things to be thankful for!

Then, two years ago, I was called back after my annual mammogram for further films. We had already returned to the island, so I had to wait over a long holiday weekend until I could have repeat films done. It was one of the longest, most stressful weekends of my life, but, finally, it ended. Then, once again, I stripped to the waist and endured the discomfort of a mammogram. A pleasant technician informed me that this time I wouldn't have to wait; they would let me know the results right away. So—I sat there. Waiting. Listening to the clock. Thinking about the possibility of breast cancer. I held, but couldn't read, a magazine and waited while a radiologist, somewhere back in the depths of radiology, looked at the films and determined my fate. The attractively furnished little waiting room was absolutely silent except for the *tick … tock … tick … tock* of the clock. Then, finally, the smiling technician opened the door and said, "Everything looks fine!"

"Thank you!" I said with a sigh of relief, and as she left the room I closed my eyes and repeated those words once again—to God.

Another "bump in the road" was when Wayne was diagnosed with Parkinson's disease five years ago, six years, to the day, after my cancer diagnosis. Once again, I could picture the worst case scenario, but with medication, his symptoms are minimized and he is managing reasonably well. Now, I find, it is my turn to be in the role of support-giver. Sometimes we feel a bit overwhelmed by the changes that aging brings about, but we learn to cope with them and try to remember to stop and give thanks that we are still here, on this beautiful earth, to experience them.

Epilogue

December 2009

So there it is. I've been one of the lucky ones—so far. I'm almost twelve years out from diagnosis now, and I'm a very thankful person. I'm not the same person I was, but that's good, I think. Being a slightly different person means that I have become more cognizant of my mortality. I realize that I need to make the most of the time I have on this earth, however long it may be. I need to take a chance now and then—try something I haven't done before, learn something new, take time to smell the fresh spring air, feel the sand between my toes on the beach, let the warm sun beat on my back, listen to the waves lapping on the shore. Most of all, however, I need to spend and enjoy time with those I love—my family and friends.

Lindquist Family on Madeline Island 2008

Also, I've come to feel that I need to do something that will ease other people's journeys through life. I suppose, in a way, I have tried to do that all my life, with my students, colleagues, family, and friends, but my awareness is heightened. I send more cards, write more e-mails, and make more phone calls just to chat, not only to take care of business. Perhaps I'm not only a different, but a better person than I was before this whole experience with cancer.

There are still times when I have a strange ache or pain that makes me wonder if cancer is lurking somewhere else in my body, but those times now come so rarely they catch me off guard. Maybe once you have had cancer you never completely get over that. Perhaps it is something that you just learn to live with. Perhaps those episodes are positive. They help you remember—not to forget. That takes me back to one of my original questions as I began to work on this project. Why would I want to remember? As I look back at all of this, I think the answer is simple. It's so I never again, for too long, take life for granted. These memories help me to appreciate each day and every breath I take. They help me to appreciate the loving family and friends that I am blessed to have. They help me to more fully appreciate the beauty and wonder of God's creation all around me. So, forget? Never! I remember. Give thanks. Celebrate. Grow. Live life to the fullest. Give as much as I can, in whatever way I can. Enjoy my grandchildren—both of them, thanks to wonderful advances in medical science, active and happy.

The danger, I see, is forgetting. It's something I have to be aware of every day. Perhaps, as my routine checkups have gotten farther apart, I have come to take them too much for granted. I now expect each time to hear that everything looks fine. I get caught up in the day-to-day routines of life—committees, choir, guests, politics, social life, decorating for holidays, and family celebrations. It's all too easy to fall back into old routines and forget the lessons that I learned in my journey through cancer.

When I feel that happening, I need to take a deep breath, step back, look at Lake Superior or the Gulf of Mexico, and talk to God. I need to just be silent—and listen. That helps me to put everything back into perspective. It makes me appreciate all that I have, and the fact that it could all be gone in a moment. Each one of us has only so many moments of life. We all need to make the most of them. Right now, perhaps because I will soon celebrate my seventy-second birthday, I seem to be in a phase where I want to leave my mark. I want people to know that I've been here, that I contributed something, and I hope that in some way I have made other lives easier. Maybe that's what it's all about—learning from each other, from our own personal struggles. If we learn from one another, perhaps we can all become stronger and more understanding people who can help to make this world a more loving and compassionate place.

If you must ever travel a similar journey, may it go well, and may you have the strength to face it. If my memories and reflections have helped in any small way, I am most thankful. I wish you a safe journey. Peace be with you!

ACKNOWLEDGMENTS

How do I begin to acknowledge all of the people who have helped to make this project become a reality? First of all, I owe a huge debt of gratitude to my husband, Wayne, a retired English professor, who encouraged me to work on this project and patiently read countless drafts and provided me with invaluable feedback and support. Our son, Eric, and daughter-in-law Susie, who are journalists, took time out of their incredibly busy lives to read this manuscript and make innumerable helpful and thoughtful suggestions, even at times correcting my recollections a bit. In addition, my dear friend and spiritual mentor, Marina Lachecki, a minister and a writer who was dealing with the terminal illness of an aging parent, took time during Lent to thoughtfully read this manuscript and give me her insights as a writer and a friend. Other old friends, Marcia Henry, Marjorie Smith, Sandi Kottke, and Melva Hisrich, also took time out of their busy lives, filled with editing, lectures, guests, and grandchildren, to read and provide me with helpful feedback. Everyone's comments didn't always agree, but each of them caught mistakes, made good suggestions and, most importantly, made me think. They have all been an important part of my life for years, and all provided me with valuable help and encouragement in the writing of this memoir. I will forever be grateful to them all!

I am also most thankful for the help of a new friend, a fellow choir member, retired nurse, and cancer survivor, Joan Hazlett. She read the manuscript and we laughed and cried together as we discussed it. Her feedback, on an emotional level, assured me that my feelings had been normal and that this was, indeed, a worthwhile project. Her encouragement and enthusiasm motivated me to keep on working, even when I was growing weary.

Family and friends mentioned above were not only there with editorial assistance with this project, but with their emotional support, as well, during my journey through cancer. Wayne was always there, even in the darkest hours, with his love and beautiful roses. Eric and Susie were as well, with their reassuring presence and thoughtful gestures, even when their hearts were full of concern for Jackson. My friends, Marina and Sandi, were also there—with a prayer, a word of encouragement, an invitation to lunch, or a bunch of flowers from their gardens. Then there was a myriad of friends, too many to name, that sent cards, made phone calls, visited, and encouraged me. All of them were there and helped to make my journey easier.

I also, of course, owe thanks to a wonderful medical team—my physicians and nurses. It was a particular joy and source of pride to see what wonderful nurses many of my former students had become, and how comfortable they could make their old professor when she was feeling vulnerable and in pain.

A *special* word, though, has to be said about the two little people who challenged and motivated me, the two who made me want to fight so hard to win the battle against cancer—my grandchildren, Katie and Jackson, those two incredible children who, I can joyfully say, I am watching grow up. They made me laugh. And cry. And most importantly, made me determined to live!

Thank you to all—family, friends, medical and nursing staff. None of you will ever truly know how much you aided me on my journey.